FOOTBALL SKILLS & TACTICS

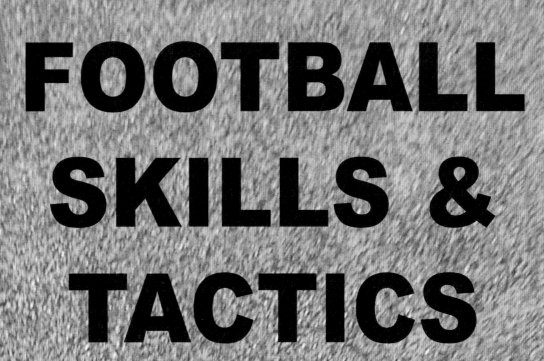

FOOTBALL SKILLS & TACTICS

Dave Smith, Pete Edwards and Adam Ward

CHANCELLOR
PRESS

Acknowledgements

The editor would like to thank Maureen Murphy and the girls of West Ham Ladies Football Club for their co-operation and patience during an icy November photoshoot. A special thank you also goes to Peter Arnold for his hard work and good humour.

Shin pads

There are a number of pictures in this book that show players without shin pads. However, it is recommended that pads be worn in all practice and match situations.

Publisher's Note

On the majority of occasions footballers have been referred to as 'he' in the book. This is simply for convenience and in no way reflects an opinion that football is a male-only sport.

Executive Editor: Julian Brown
Senior Editor: Trevor Davies
Creative Director: Keith Martin
Design Manager: Bryan Dunn
Senior Designer: Peter Burt
Design: Martin Topping
Picture Research: Rosie Garai
Production Controller: Sarah Scanlon

Artworks produced by Kevin Jones Associates

First published in Great Britain in 2000
by Hamlyn, an imprint of Octopus Publishing Group Limited

Published 2002 by Chancellor Press, an imprint of Bounty Books,
a division of Octopus Publishing Group Limited.

This hardback edition published 2003 by Chancellor Press,
an imprint of Bounty Books, a division of
Octopus Publishing Group Limited,
2 - 4 Heron Quays,London E14 4JP

Reprinted 2004, 2005

ISBN 0 7537 0749 7
ISBN 13 9 780753 707494

A catalogue record for this book is available from the British Library

Printed in China

introduction

Football may be the 'world's best loved game', but it is also an extremely competitive sport where mediocrity has no place. Whatever level you play the game at, you owe it to yourself and your team-mates to hone your skills and fitness to the maximum. Play the game half-heartedly and you will soon get found out.

The techniques and tactics outlined in the next 153 pages should go some way to helping you make the most of your talent. Each chapter deals with a key area of the game, from the first, painful stretches of the pre-season build-up to the very latest theories on tactics and strategies.

According to the world's top coaches, the two most important ingredients in a footballer are fitness and skill. It is impossible to say which is more important, so it is essential that all players work at both. Fortunately, this book includes a chapter on fitness that will help you avoid the frustrating situation where your legs refuse to do what your brain asks them to do. And with sections on both basic and more advanced ball skills, your brain should at least get the instructions to your legs right.

Football is of course a game that was invented to give pleasure, and the better one plays it, the more pleasure it brings. Anyone who doubts this, should read Pele's description of the first goal he scored in the World Cup finals, as a 17-year-old against Wales:

'I have no idea how many times I ran and jumped, ran and jumped, all the while screaming "GOOOOOOAAAAAAALLLLLL!!!!!!!" like a maniac. I had to get rid of that tremendous pressure of relief, of joy, of I don't know what was inside me! I was crying like a baby, babbling, while the rest of the team pummelled me, almost suffocating me. That was certainly my most unforgettable goal..."

Pele enjoyed the experience so much that he went on to score around 1300 more!

FiTNESS AND TRAiNiNG

1

Fitness training is often the most effective way for a footballer to improve his game. By increasing your stamina you can eliminate the frustrating scenario in which your brain tells you to make a run but your legs are unable to comply. Being fit to compete for 90 minutes is no mean feat. It takes discipline, dedication and many hours on the training ground. However, for those who persevere the rewards are worthwhile.

① Diet

●**All things in moderation – even burgers. But don't let treats dominate your diet.**

Striking a balance

The days of rump steak for a pre-match meal and fish and chips as a post-match top-up are long gone in the professional game. Nowadays, most top clubs employ dietitians who are responsible for ensuring that players eat a 'balanced diet'. To achieve peak performance, footballers must follow a diet that strikes a balance between carbohydrate, fat and protein.

Fats

Fat has double the calories of carbohydrate and protein but that doesn't mean it gives you more energy. Nothing, in fact, could be further from the truth. Fat in itself is something the body uses slowly – storing any surplus in various parts of the body. Meat, dairy products and even some fruit such as avocado provide abundant sources of fat.

Carbohydrates

Carbohydrate (or carbs to use the jargon of sports science) is the fuel on which your body runs. Good sources of carbohydrate include potatoes, pasta, rice and bread. Carbohydrate is converted into glycogen, which is stored in the liver and to a lesser extent the muscles until it is carried in the blood to muscle cells during exercise. The relative calories (and therefore food) burned during activity depend on the fitness and metabolism of the individual and the intensity and duration of the exercise. To be sure you have plenty of carbohydrate available for your glycogen stores, you should eat regular meals – particularly in the three days leading up to a match when it is best to eat four small meals a day.

Proteins

Protein is used for building muscle and is vital for growth and to maintain health. But because it takes a long time to digest, it is not a source of immediate energy. You need a regular supply of protein, although not as much as you might think. You don't want protein with lots of fat (such as red meat and dairy products). Better protein sources are white poultry meat, fish and soya beans.

Vitamins and supplements

Providing you eat plenty of fresh fruit and vegetables, you do not need to worry about your vitamin intake. The vitamins you need plenty of are A (found in vegetables including spinach, carrots and sweetcorn), C (found in fruit and fruit juice) and E (found in nuts, seeds and whole grains). If you feel that you need to supplement your diet you can do so with extra vitamins in the form of tablets. However, all youngsters should check with their parents before taking any tablets of any kind.

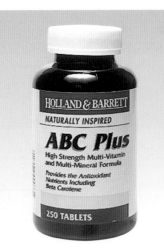

●**If you know you don't eat a balanced diet, make the effort and keep yourself healthy by taking regular supplements. There are many different types available, including special varieties for athletes and vegetarians.**

If you don't eat the right things at the right times you won't get the best out of your body. To achieve peak fitness it is essential to follow a strict dietary code. Sure, let yourself go every now and again by tucking into a rich slap-up meal but don't do anything to excess and enjoy your 'treats' in moderation. For a number of years players in Italy have enjoyed specially designed diets according to their individual needs. This approach is now being adopted throughout the world and at every level of the game.

Protein sources

- Meat
- Fish
- Cheese
- Eggs
- Soya
- Nuts

Carbohydrate sources

- Potatoes
- Whole grain products
- Rice
- Pasta
- Dried fruit
- Starchy food

Fat sources

- Milk products
- Nuts
- Fish
- Meat

Dos and Don'ts

Do...
... increase your intake of complex carbohydrates (pasta, rice, etc.) three days before playing.
... drink isotonic drinks free from sodium.
... follow a sensible diet at all times – not just prior to a big match.

Don't...
... add fat to your food, e.g. butter on jacket potatoes.
... drink tea or coffee at half-time. – both of these drinks are diuretic and drain fluid rather than replace it.
... eat burgers, chocolate or other foods containing saturated fat prior to a match. These foods should only ever be eaten as occasional treats.

● Carbohydrates should dominate an athlete's diet. Pasta is a popular choice, but avoid creamy sauces that have a high fat content.

A professional diet

Footballers have to be disciplined with their food, but they don't have to live like monks. You can go out and have a decent meal in the evening providing the rest of your day you haven't been eating and drinking rubbish. A healthy and typical diet for a professional footballer would contain plenty of carbohydrate, for example:

Breakfast
Cereal, half a pint of skimmed milk, bread and preserve. Orange juice.

Lunch (after training)
A meal high in complex carbohydrates with a small intake of protein. Chicken with rice or jacket potato and green vegetables. Pasta is also popular. This will be followed by fruit with an isotonic drink. If players are training in the afternoon they will eat smaller portions but the meal will still be based around carbohydrates.

Evening meal
As with lunch, the evening meal should be made up of foods high in carbohydrates. This meal should also contain protein too. Fish and chicken with rice, boiled potatoes, vegetables or pasta are all popular.

If you eat the wrong things three days before a game it can be just as harmful to your performance as a poor pre-match meal. On the other hand, if you eat plenty of carbohydrate three days before a game your muscles will be fuelled when you come to play. However, you must eat the right kind of carbohydrate. Complex carbohydrates together with a little fat and a little protein should be eaten for the three days prior to a game. On the day of the game itself eat carbs that give instant fuel. Popular foods include light pasta, cereal and whole grain products.

Post-match refuelling

Research has shown that footballers' glycogen levels can be down as much as 75 per cent after a game and those levels have to be restored to normal as soon as possible. At top professional clubs a chef travels everywhere with the team. He, or she, ensures that players eat the correct foods both before and after a match. You have two to five hours to replace your glycogen stores after a game and it is crucial that you eat the right things. Try to eat plenty of carbohydrate after the game; eating junk food will undo all of your good pre-match preparation.

Fluids

The human body is made up of 80 per cent fluid. Some of this fluid is lost every time you exercise. To keep healthy and fit fluids must be replaced. Footballers should drink at least half a litre of water before and after a warm-up. It is also a good idea to consume an isotonic drink before playing a game. Tea, coffee, alcohol and any drinks containing caffeine should be avoided.

Isotonic drinks

Isotonic drinks are easily absorbed into the blood stream and provide quicker rehydration than water. There are many specially designed isotonic drinks on the market, but a simple isotonic solution can be made by mixing equal quantities of fruit juice and water.

Carbo loading

● Three days before a game players should start 'carbo loading'. That is to say, that 75 per cent of food eaten should be complex carbohydrates. Four small meals a day are consumed, rather than two, as the body absorbs smaller amounts more efficiently than huge portions.

During a competitive football match, a player will work at a rate in excess of 75 per cent of maximum fitness. Training sessions must reflect this, and should be organised to work players as hard as if they were playing a match. Once you have achieved a base level of fitness in pre-season, the priority should be to build lung and aerobic capacity and develop the strength and power in the leg muscles.

You do not need to be able to run a marathon to be fit for football. In most cases, it is better to run a shorter distance at a greater pace than to set off on a time-consuming long jog. Try to run at a pace that increases your fitness level. For stamina work, players should start off running distances of up to one

● **Running is the key to building stamina for football. To achieve a high level of fitness, however, such exercise must be combined with appropriate recovery periods.**

● **Short, high-intensity runs are an important part of pre-season training. Each run should be followed by a period of recovery. Here, players sprint for 25m, turn and walk back for 25m (recovery) and then repeat six times.**

No matter how agile or skilful a player is, he or she will be letting the side down if their contribution is not maintained throughout the 90 minutes. Players who can't stay the course soon find themselves out of the game. Stamina is the answer, but this highly-prized commodity does not come easily... it takes hard work and more hard work.

mile (1.6km) and increase the length of the run as they feel able. Repeats of shorter runs are also useful. A professional session might involve running three repeats of 900m, followed by three repeats of 600m and finished off with three repeats of 300m. each run would be separated by a 2.5 minute break.

This type of running should be punctuated with ball work – ideally small-sided games. The running and the practice game should complement one another – if the running is high intensity (see page 28) then the game should be moderate intensity (see page 30) and vice versa. Whichever combination you choose, make sure the lower intensity work is done last as this can form part of the overall warm-down.

Hill running

Hill running is one of the most effective but painful ways of building your powers of endurance as well as your lactic tolerance. Find a hill which really works your leg muscles when you run up it, but don't go for a monster – a 30 per cent gradient will only demoralise you. When you've settled on a hill, run short repeats. Hill repeats of eight to 21 seconds are recommended. The following schedule will provide a vigorous work-out:

1. 3 x 21-second repeats
2. 3 x 15-second repeats
3. 3 x 8-second repeats

When you have achieved a decent level of base fitness, you can safely increase your speed, as you progress through the repeats, without risking injury. It is essential to stretch properly before hill work. It is an exercise that puts a great strain on your body, so prepare properly.

Recovery time

When building stamina during pre-season, or after any extended break from football, it is essential to give your body time to recover between sessions. You can't do a long run one day and do an even longer run the next. It doesn't work that way. You have to do things over an extended period with sufficient rest in between exertions. A common problem is that players try to top up their fitness programme daily. All they do is come to a point where they are so fatigued that they go backwards. Give yourself adequate time to recover.

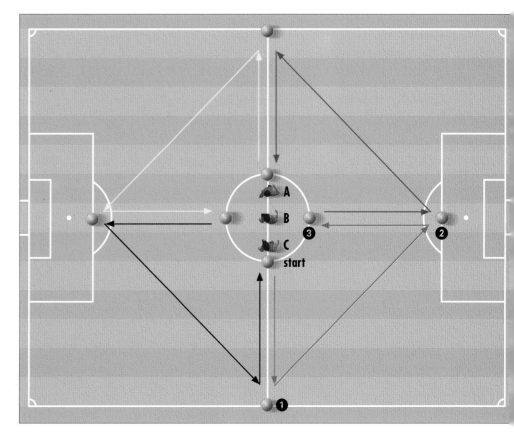

Summer tip

● Low impact aerobic exercise can break the monotony of training during the summer. Cycling and swimming are excellent ways to keep fit and involve very low risk of injury. Keep a close eye on your weight and three weeks before returning to football step up our own personal training programme.

● Player A sets off sprinting to mark ❶, when he gets there Player B sets off in pursuit, when B reaches mark ❶ player C sets off. All players continue their runs unbroken to mark ❸. As soon as all three players are at mark ❸ they set off (staggered as before) on run two. This exercise is repeated until all players are back at the start.

Throughout the professional game warming-up is taken very seriously, but whatever level you play at, there is no reason why you can't go through a short but thorough warm-up and stretching routine. Prepare properly and you give yourself a better chance of performing to the best of your ability for the duration of a game. Warming-up for a training session or match should start with light stretching for 15 minutes. This should be followed by light running which will get the body temperature and heart rate up. Continue the warm-up until you are breathing heavily and your muscles feel fully stretched.

Top to bottom stretching

Legs are an outfield player's most important tools. But when warming-up, don't forget the top half of your body. It is vital that the whole body is warm, supple and prepared for exercise. A top to bottom warm-up – starting with the upper body and hips, and finishing with the calf muscles and Achilles tendons – is the best way to get your body properly prepared for the rigours of exercise. Before you begin any stretching, however, it is advisable to jog gently around the pitch or training field for a few minutes to raise the body temperature and your heart rate. Don't do anything excessive and always remember you shouldn't stretch a muscle that is cold.

Lower body

Soccer players are more susceptible to groin strains than most sportsmen. The groin muscles, which are located on the inside of the thigh, can be damaged when a player over-stretches, or stretches awkwardly, for a ball or tackle. In some cases groin injuries are unavoidable. But the better you prepare your body the greater the chance of avoiding injury.

On your marks

This is an exaggerated version of a sprinter's starting position. The following muscles are stretched by this exercise – frontal groin area, thigh, calf and Achilles. Adopt the position of an elevated press-up, with your arms shoulder-width apart for support, and then bring one foot up between your hands. Dip your body weight towards the ground from the waist. Hold and repeat bringing your other foot forward.

Whether you're warming-up before a game or a training session, you should take the time to stretch properly and ensure your body is supple enough to perform at its peak. It is also essential to warm-down after exercise. If you don't stretch properly, your chances of getting injured will be far greater – especially on a cold day.

Hamstring

The hamstring (or the rear leg bicep to be more accurate) is located at the back of the leg. It is a muscle group which travels all the way from the lower buttock to the back of the knee. As anyone who has suffered a hamstring tear (sprint athletes and speedy wingers are particularly susceptible) will tell you, this injury is extremely painful. Hamstring injuries always occur suddenly (it's like an elastic band snapping) and, while there can be no guaranteed protection, good stretching is the soundest precaution you can take. Stretching your hamstrings will also make you more flexible, helping you get into more exaggerated positions.

The floor splits

● This exercise is one which many people will be unable to complete fully. If that is the case, start with your legs closer together and only take your head down a short way. Gradually widen your legs, pushing your head down towards the ground or towards your knees. Go wider and deeper the more flexible you become.

⑤ Suppleness

The frontal quad

The frontal quad is a very large muscle in the thigh. It is one of the easiest to pull and one of the most difficult to heal. Muscle strains are common, particularly when players are pushing off from a standing start. The thigh can even take a number of direct blows during a game. Pain and tension in the thigh can also be the result of a problem elsewhere – typically this is caused by problems in the knee or the pelvis. Good all round flexibility reduces the chance of strains, but it cannot legislate for a clumsy defender's knee going straight into your thigh. All you can do is prime your muscles by stretching properly.

Thigh stretch

Before you carry out this exercise, always do some basic stretching first. Even then, you should only try this stretch if are a flexible person. Adopt the position as shown, using your left arm as support and your right arm to pull back your left leg. Try to keep your body at a 45-degree angle. Hold this position for ten seconds and then repeat to stretch the other leg. Always pull your leg straight back and not at an angle when attempting this exercise.

The lower leg

The most likely muscle to be affected by cramp is the calf muscle. Most footballers know the pain of cramp in the calf only too well. The causes of cramp are the subject of much debate. Obstruction of blood/oxygen supply, salt deficiency or deficiency of other body minerals have all been blamed. All no doubt play their part, but muscle fatigue due to prolonged work is clearly a major culprit. Development and preparation of the calf muscle will limit the chances of cramp. The calf and Achilles tendon are closely linked and often a pain in the Achilles is the result of a blow to the calf muscle. The lower leg is a very sensitive area and, therefore, requires special attention. The Achilles tendon, for example, should not be stretched too quickly or too strenuously. The ankle meanwhile is a very strong joint but, as it takes most of the force if the foot lands at an unexpected angle, the sprained ankle is the most common sports injury. 'Going over' on an ankle is very painful and results in damage to the ankle ligaments which will take about six weeks to heal. Suppleness in this area of the body is essential.

Calf and Achilles stretch

This exercise stretches the calf and Achilles. It may look awkward, but it is worth practising and getting right. Position your weight on the bent, rear leg while the front leg provides extra support. Keep your weight central and do not lean too far forward. Hold this position for 20 seconds and then repeat for the other leg.

Tips

- Don't rush into any stretching exercise. Ease yourself into the stretch gently and listen to your body
- Always hold a stable, balanced body position. Uneven weight distribution will make exercises more difficult and less effective
- Avoid sharp, sudden movements. Keep your stretching smooth and you won't get injured in the warm-up
- Breathe in through your nose and exhale through your mouth as you work through the exercise. Do not hold your breath at any point during the exercise

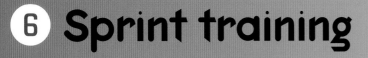

Football is a game that requires both aerobic and anaerobic fitness. For parts of a game you will work anaerobically – most commonly this will come in the form of short sprints, during which you will build up an oxygen debt and lactic acid in your muscles. These periods are followed by longer spells of jogging and walking. However, at any time during a game you must be ready to enter oxygen debt and go anaerobic.

In order to sustain these periods of exertion, you must build up your tolerance to anaerobic exercise by working it into your training schedule. In this way your body will be better prepared to adapt and cope with high-intensity exercise and lactate pressure. You will also reduce your recovery time... not to mention your desire to stand with your hands on your hips, gasping for air after a 30m run. If you are going to compete for 90 minutes, you have to expose yourself to anaerobic exercise in your training.

● Pictures 1–3 illustrate a simple exercise which helps to improve speed, reaction and acceleration. The coach (in red) directs the players with a shout to move left (1) via an exaggerated step, then move right (2) via a similar step and then finally to accelerate straight ahead (3). This exercise can be repeated several times, or alternatively incorporated into a longer run.

The term anaerobic means 'without air' and is used to describe exercise which is intense, such as sprinting or weight training. It is inefficient, compared to aerobic activity, and requires you to work your heart very hard. Anaerobic activity cannot be sustained for long periods.

● Shuttle runs are an excellent form of sprint training. Short bursts of sprinting are followed by periods of recovery before the run is repeated.

Short-burst training will improve your anaerobic fitness. Sprints of between five and ten seconds, followed by a walk back to the starting point and several repeats, are ideal. Players should work to their maximum capacity for these short periods. This sort of work helps increase your lactate threshold.

The danger with anaerobic training is that there is a high risk of injury because you are pushing yourself so hard. For this reason, you should not do this type of exercise too often. Use it occasionally, perhaps only once every 2–3 weeks, in order to supplement your regular training programme. If your body can cope with this sort of high-intensity work-out, you have a better chance of making that 50m surge in the last few minutes of a game.

● The ability to make a quick run at the end of a tiring game is a major asset to any player. Training exercises aimed at building this type of speed endurance require the player to work against resistance. Here the coach is holding the player back by a tape worn across his midriff. Other speed endurance exercises employ weighted jackets to get players working hard.

Jargon Buster

● Anaerobic training involves short, quick bursts – between five and seven seconds. Sprint up, walk back and sprint again
● Aerobic training involves longer runs – anything over 15 seconds. You run and then warm-down

7 Plyometric training

Plyometric training helps develop explosive power within the muscles and there are various ways of achieving this. The most common methods use hurdles, benches and hoops for hopping, jumping and side-stepping with an explosive action. This type of exercise stimulates the mytatic reflex (the sort of reaction you get when someone touches your arm with a recently extinguished match).

Plyometric training will help you to turn more quickly and get away from opponents. It will also give you a little extra explosive pace which can make a great difference. Even if you are not blessed with great speed, by improving your plyometric fitness, you will be able to compete with the fastest player over that all-important first yard. This sort of training also improves agility and co-ordination, thus enabling you to change direction quickly – a major benefit in the modern game.

● A great deal of plyometric training uses hurdles to help sharpen reactions within the muscles. This exercise requires players to put on a weighted jacket, before jumping on the spot (with knees up high and hands on hips as shown) five times. The player then removes the weighted jacket, jumps the five hurdles, puts on the weighted jacket once more, runs on the spot for 10 seconds and then turns sharply and sprints back to the starting position. This exercise improves not only plyometric fitness, but also speed and speed endurance.

Plyometrics is not about speed over distance... it is about improving that critical, initial burst of acceleration.

Plyometric training must be carried out on a soft surface. There is a big shock or impact factor involved in this kind of explosive training and it is important to take precautions against injury (jarring of the knee, twisting of the ankle, etc.). Ideally you should use either grass, or a training mat in a gym. It is also essential to wear shoes that offer both support and cushioning.

When working in this way it is important to be thoroughly warmed up beforehand – just as you would be before a game. Training sessions which involve plyometrics should last no more than 20 minutes and should be carried out no more than twice a week. Any more than this and you are making excessive demands of your body and increasing the risk of injury. Train hard, but train sensibly – and allow yourself adequate recovery time in between.

● Jumping over hurdles is a great way to improve plyometric fitness. This type of training should only be used occasionally and for short periods however. Try to vary the exercises – jumping hurdles from side to side (red shirt) for example.

Goalkeeper training varies dramatically from that of outfield players, although the same fitness principles still apply. Keepers have to be more agile and need quicker reflexes than a typical outfield player. To this end, keepers need to do a lot of plyometric work, ideally using hurdles and weighted jackets in their training.

Goalkeepers must also do a great deal of stretching work too. All good keepers are flexible – if they're not, they get injured. A keeper has to get into some awkward positions and it's important he doesn't pull a muscle while stretching for an awkward ball.

Strength work in the gym should form an important part of a professional keeper's training. Upper body strength is a valuable commodity between the posts, as keepers have to withstand many physical challenges during a typical game.

Goalies have to be quick off the mark and alert, which means they must carry minimal body fat. They will generally be more muscular than outfield players, particularly in their legs, which have to supply the power and spring to reach high balls. Plyometric training will help to improve a keeper's spring.

Diet and playing in goal

Goalkeepers do not do as much aerobic activity as outfield players and for this reason, they must take great care about what they eat. An hour and a half between the posts will not burn off a portion of fish and chips or an extra slice of chocolate cake. It is essential that keepers stay trim; the more weight they are carrying the more they have got to work to spring and jump. Power-weight ratios are just as important to keepers as they are to outfield players. A good healthy diet with a large proportion of carbohydrate will help prevent weight gain and sluggish goalkeeping.

Goalkeepers are so often the forgotten men when it comes to training, but their fitness is just as important as that of any outfield player. Traditionally, goalkeeper training involved hitting a few crosses and shots at the keeper after he'd spent an hour or so running around a field. Nowadays professional keepers receive special training to improve their reactions, their speed off the line, their kicking and the other skills that make the difference between three points won or lost. This approach should be adopted at all levels of the game.

● This exercise helps to improve both reactions and speed off the line. Five balls are spaced in an arc around the six yard box and each ball is numbered. The coach then stands on the penalty spot and throws balls at the keeper to save (1). At any point during the exercise (and without warning) the coach shouts out a number and the keeper must dive onto the corresponding ball (2-3). The coach resumes throwing balls from the penalty spot immediately.

A balanced routine

Ideally, keepers should divide their training time between the training ground and the gym. Time in the gym should be spent building up body strength. Springing exercises on the benches and squats will also help improve agility. Speed (over short distances) and strength are closely related. If a keeper works hard on his strength, he will be quick off his line.

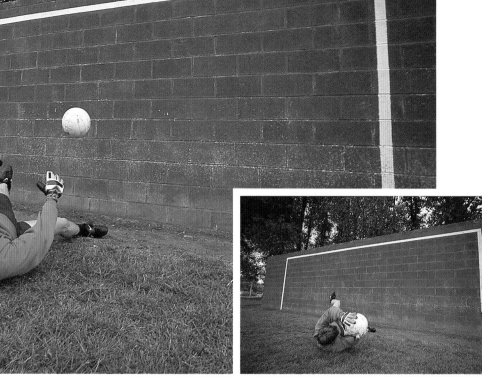

Warm-up

A keeper's warm-up should be slightly different to that of an outfield player. Greater emphasis is placed on stretching – particularly the arms and upper body. It is imperative to warm-up properly, especially in the winter when strains can occur if the muscles aren't prepared properly. By the same token, if you are lucky enough to play for a team where you have nothing to do for long periods, you should stretch throughout the game. However, always keep an eye on what's going on at the other end!

● Reactions and handling skills can be improved by lying in front of a wall, throwing the ball against the wall and diving to save it as it rebounds towards you. Try to speed up as you get more confident; throwing the ball harder and harder each time. Ideally you should try to direct your throws so that you work on saves to both the left and right sides.

● The art of goalkeeping is not just about getting your hands to the ball, it's about getting enough power in your save to protect your goal. The exercise shown above helps develop the keeper's spring and push, by forcing him to dive over a rope (held by the player kneeling down). The coach throws the ball to one side of the rope and then, before the keeper has had time to recover properly, throws one to the other side. This improves the keeper's reactions.

Note: The rope should always be held low down and must be held relaxed enough to avoid injury to the keeper if he catches himself on it.

The mental game

At professional level, keepers work with a specific goalkeeper coach for several days a week. The coach will work on the player's handling, but will also try and build confidence. If a keeper loses his confidence, the whole team are in trouble, so it is important that training sessions do not demoralise goalkeepers. Concentration is another essential element in a keeper's game, but the only way to improve this is to play plenty of practice matches.

Tip

● A popular routine used by top keepers is to stand in a circle of discs, each of which has a different number. The coach calls out a number and the keeper has to run to that disc, dive on it, run back to the centre of the circle and then go again

Warm-up

As with any type of football training, it is important to carry out a proper warm-up before beginning a high-intensity session. If you are planning a high-intensity training session, then a high-intensity warm-up should precede it. The body will be warm, the muscles prepared and the heart rate reaching a level needed for the sort of hard work which follows. A high-intensity session will replicate the exertions of a proper match, so your warm-up should be the same as your pre-match preparation.

Hard but not too hard

● Small-sided games are an excellent and enjoyable form of high-intensity training. Try to make sure that all players are working hard during the session and get the ball into play quickly when it goes outside the playing area.

The majority of high-intensity training takes the form of small-sided games, although exercises can be done without the ball. Either way, the aim is to keep the body working at a high heart rate. However, it's not about pushing yourself until you drop. Running until you collapse through exhaustion is not the way ahead. All you are doing is knocking your legs out. The idea is to push yourself, but not kill yourself.

The aim of high-intensity training is to keep the heart rate high and the body working at a level which simulates a match situation. A player will work in excess of 75 per cent of his maximum capacity during a match. High-intensity training should reflect this – albeit for shorter periods. In some cases, training should be more physically demanding than a match, with players working at up to 95 per cent of their maximum. By pushing themselves over and above what they'd expect to do in a match, those last gruelling 15 minutes of a game won't be so bad.

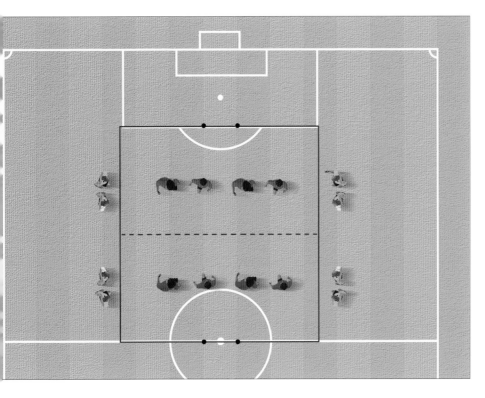

Team A

Team B

● Goalposts

- - - - Shooting line

Players resting from teams C + D. Their job is to get the ball back into the playzone quickly

● This high-intensity four v four game uses a small area of pitch with resting players standing around the playing area ready to get the ball back into play should it go 'dead'. There are no goalkeepers, but shooting is only allowed within a marked area. After five minutes the players on the outside swap with those in the 'play-zone'.

High-intensity session

An ideal session would comprise some short sprint work (short runs with six repeats) but, in the main, would be built around various small-sided games. An example of this is a four v four practice match on a small pitch with eight other players standing around the pitch, acting as a wall to keep the ball in play and keep the intensity as high as possible. These games last 4–8 minutes. At the end of this period, the players rotate with those standing on the outside of the pitch. In total, the session should last no longer than 45 minutes.

Recovery

It is essential to give the body enough time to recover between high-intensity exercises or games. If you are working without the ball, for example, you should train for 8–12 minutes and then allow 2–3 minutes for rest before starting work again. This process can be continued for about an hour – though no longer. High-intensity training is an excellent way for older players to maintain their fitness. However, it is important to take an extended recovery period between exercises.

● It is imperative that high-intensity sessions contain enough time for players to recover. Without recovery time, fitness will be eroded rather than developed. As a rough guide, you should allow three minutes of rest for every 10 minutes of exertion.

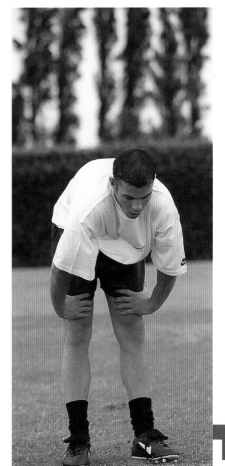

11 Moderate and low intensity training

Moderate -intensity games

A typical moderate-intensity session would begin with a warm-up and stretch – this does not need to be as vigorous as the high-intensity warm-up, as the pulse will not be taken to such a high level during the session. When warm, players divide into teams and prepare for a small-sided game. There are many variations of low-intensity small-sided games, but all have one aim…to restrict the movement and pace of the game. This can be achieved by playing on a larger pitch, but marking the playing area into zones which players cannot move from. Alternatively, players can be restricted to three touches in certain areas and free football in others, which can be coupled with restrictions being placed upon players going into certain areas of the pitch in an effort to prevent them over-stretching themselves. As with the high-intensity games, sessions should last around 45 minutes. Players should not exert themselves too much during these games, although you can back the game up with some moderate-intensity running. Other examples of moderate or low-intensity games include head tennis or possession games involving a handful of players in a circle.

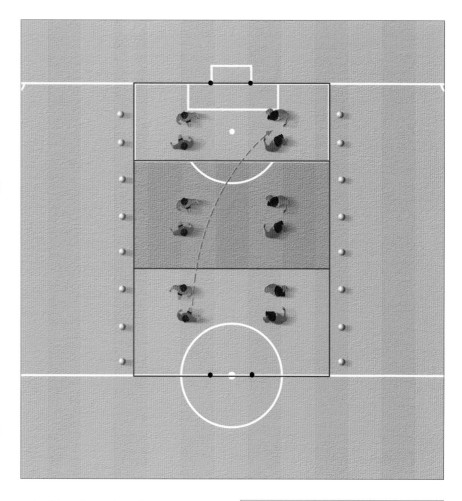

● In this moderate-intensity game, players are restricted to particular areas to limit their exertion while tackling is not allowed in the middle third of the pitch. Passes are allowed between any zones (as illustrated) and balls are ready on the sidelines to keep the game running.

Team A	
Team B	
●	Goalposts
- - - -	Pass
▨	Walk zone, no tackling
●	Footballs

For training after a game or after a high-intensity work-out, a moderate-intensity session is ideal. The body needs time to recover from a hard work-out, and it is counterproductive to have two high-intensity sessions back-to-back. This leads to over-tiredness and the risk of injuries. A moderate session, as the name implies, involves a reasonable work-out but does not push the body to the sort of levels of exertion involved in a high-intensity session. These sessions are purely aerobic; players are not required to work their hearts hard or go into oxygen debt.

● Above: The red player shadows his opponent, while the players outside the zone wait for the play to move to them.

● Left: Low-intensity small-sided game. In this exercise, players are restricted to particular areas, there is no tackling (just shadowing) and levels of exertions are kept right down.

Low-intensity games

Low-intensity sessions usually involve squaring off an area of the training field, dividing it up into areas from which players are not allowed to move, and playing a small-sided game. Players cannot travel – or pass the ball in certain cases – from zone to zone. In this way, the game is played at little more than a jogging pace. This type of game can be used to help to lower the intensity gradually after a strenuous session. In doing so, it helps the recovery process. Low-intensity games based around full-sized games are also used in the run up to matches. These games are usually punctuated by discussions about tactics and set plays.

● Head tennis is a good form of low-intensity training. The emphasis is on developing technique, but it still makes players concentrate and work a little too.

The benefits of warm-up

Do not underestimate the importance of warming-up before training or playing. The benefits of following a good warm-up routine based around a comprehensive programme of stretches are twofold:

1. You will increase your performance at the start of a game or practice session
2. You will decrease your risk of injury.

There is also a psychological benefit to be gained from a thorough warm-up. If you feel that you are properly prepared, you will be confident and raring to go at the start of a game. Time spent warming-up can also help you focus on what lies ahead – composure is a valuable commodity at the start of a football match. Warming-up can even help to relax tense and nervous players prior to kick-off.

A 15-minute warm-up will ensure you're properly prepared, but if you fail to warm-up for long enough the results can be disastrous. Even if you are fortunate enough to get through the game without picking up an injury, you will be unable to perform at your maximum level from the start of the game. For the first 10–15 minutes, you will effectively be warming-up.

Stretch your muscles

A good warm-up will gradually increase the blood flow in your body, raising the temperature of the muscles and improving their flexibility. Muscle temperature reaches a suitable level after about ten minutes, which is why it is recommended that the warm-up period should last between 10 and 15 minutes and certainly no longer than 20. In effect, your warm-up will get your body into an aerobic state to withstand strenuous, physical exercise. If you try to warm-up during the fast and frantic opening 15 minutes of a game, you will place a tremendous strain on your muscles. Injuries occur when the muscles have not been sufficiently warmed up. A cold muscle is more rigid and a sudden or rapid movement means it is unable to respond quickly enough and can tear. However, when a muscle is raised in temperature, its performance and flexibility are enhanced by around 20 per cent.

● **The three exercises shown below will get your heart-rate up and are a good framework around which to build your warm-up:**
1. **Kick your knees up high, using your hands as a guide.**
2. **Flick your heels up to touch your hands as you run.**
3. **Twist the top of your body and run side-steps, alternating to face both ways.**

1

2

3

Warm-up is not just something for the pros. Whatever level you play the game at, you owe it to yourself and your team-mates to prepare your body properly for the exertions to come.

A warm heart

The warm-up also helps take your heart rate from a relaxed state up to a level at which it is ready for work. That level should be something in the region of 120 beats per minute. As the heart rate goes up and the flow of blood around the body increases, your muscles produce heat. As the intensity of the warm-up is raised, more heat is generated and some is transferred from the muscles into the blood and dispersed throughout the body.

Wasted warm-ups

Once you have completed your pre-match warm-up, do not return to the dressing room and put your feet up before going back out for the kick-off. This will waste all the work you have just done – your heart rate will drop and your muscles will grow colder and less flexible. Instead, you should keep your body warm – jogging on the spot or continued stretching will work. So keep the body moving, particularly during winter months when warm-up takes on a whole new importance.

Winter warm-ups

When the weather is hot, your body temperature and muscles respond quicker than during colder weather. During the winter months it is essential to warm-up with plenty of layers of clothes on. Only remove your layers when you are sufficiently warm. Don't try to warm-up in just your playing kit when it's freezing cold – you will not be able to get sufficiently warm. On very cold days, try to warm-up inside and only venture out onto the pitch when you have to.

Playing outdoor football in the winter always involves a risk of injury, so it is as well to train in a gym, doing weights or playing indoor five-a-side. Avoid going out in freezing cold temperatures if you can. But always be prepared to work yourself hard when training inside during these cold periods. Don't use the weather as an excuse to take it easy.

On the bench

If you are on the substitutes bench, you should still warm-up as if you are starting the game. You never know when you will be needed. During the first half of the game, subs should jog and stretch every ten minutes or so. Warm-up for 15 minutes straight after half-time and every ten minutes after that until you are needed.

● **An organised team warm-up will ensure every one is prepared for the start of the game. It can also fill the opposition with fear. Here the players run towards the coach (in red) kicking their knees up and then turn and run away from him, flicking their heels up as they go.**

BASiC SKiLLS 2

According to the famous cliché, you shouldn't try to 'run before you can walk'. However, in the case of football this saying can be adapted to read, 'don't try to kick 'til you can trap'. Time spent mastering the basics is well spent, and will undoubtedly stand you in good stead when you later try to develop your repertoire of skills. In any case, it is the fundamental arts of ball control, passing, tackling and heading that dominate the average game of football, rather then any more sophisticated skills. Master the basics and you will be an asset to any team.

● To make a good contact with the ball, you must get your body into a good position as you approach it. This will maintain the correct body shape throughout the strike resulting in a deliberate follow through and, most importantly, an accurate kick.

When kicking a ball

1. Avoid using your toe unless you have no other alternative.
2. When possible, try to use the inside, outside, top or instep of the boot.
3. For the greatest degree of accuracy when passing or controlling the ball use the inside of the foot (see right).
4. It is important to practise using both feet and not be dependent on one strong foot.
5. Position your non-kicking foot correctly. It should always be next to the ball as it is struck and not ahead of or behind the ball. The position of your non-kicking foot determines the balance and power you generate.
6. Practise regularly and try to master the different ways – inside, outside or instep – of striking the ball. Using both feet too.
7. Check where you are aiming the ball before striking, but remember to keep your eye on the ball when making the kick.

If you can't kick a ball correctly, you're not going to go too far as a footballer. You may think this is obvious but, for many people, the most simple and basic aspect of the game does not come naturally. For some players it needs a lot of practice. The more you play football, the more you realise the importance of keeping possession – the art of passing the ball to a team-mate with good weight and accuracy. To achieve that you need to feel comfortable with the ball at your feet and know when and how to deliver the ball to a colleague.

The top
The most powerful contact area of the boot. The sweet spot, as some like to call it. Used for driving the ball long distances, shooting or clearing.

The inside
Probably the first area of the foot you will use for kicking. Used for controlling and passing the ball with the greatest degree of accuracy.

The outside
Used for bending or swerving the ball around opponents, normally from dead-ball situations.

The instep
Used more often than any other part of the foot. Passing, crossing, chipping, shooting; the instep is used in the execution of all these arts.

Kicking areas of the foot

 **First touch**

The side of the foot

This is the most simple and effective method of controlling the ball. If it is carried out correctly the ball will come to rest close enough for you to make your next move. All players should be able to control the ball with either foot using this technique.

● Get in position early and try not to put all your weight through your standing leg. If you stand lightly on the balls of your feet, you will be able to adjust if the ball bounces awkwardly.

● Watch the ball onto the large area of the foot and cushion the impact by pulling your foot back slightly.

● Try to guide the ball into your stride rather than at your feet. If it finishes too close, you will be forced to take a step back before passing or shooting.

Practice

When it comes to honing your first touch, the old methods are the best. If you are practising alone, find a wall to work on and strike the ball at various heights, speeds and angles to test your control. If you have a partner, you can practise by throwing or kicking the ball to each other. Remember to work on all the different ways of bringing the ball under control.

First touch is vital. Watch any good player and you will quickly see the benefits of a true first touch. The top stars bring the ball under control in an instant and, as a result, have time to consider their next move. But whatever level of the game you play at, you cannot afford to waste time chasing miscontrolled passes. So rather than let yourself and your team-mates down, practise the fundamental art of ball control and develop your first touch.

Sole of the foot

The trap with the sole of the foot - often used to bring a bouncing ball to a standstill – is not as easy as it looks. A split-second lapse in concentration will result in the ball sliding underneath your foot, so keep your eyes on the ball at all times. Bring your controlling foot down gently, yet positively, onto the ball. Do not stamp as this could result in the ball squirting from beneath your foot and out of your possession.

● A perfectly executed trap. The ball has been brought under control with the sole of the player's right boot. The only drawback with this technique is that the ball ends up literally under the feet of the player, forcing him to take a step back before shooting or passing.

Dos and Don'ts

1. Do practise with both feet
2. Don't take your eye off the ball
3. Do use the side-foot trap wherever possible
4. Don't start looking at where you're going to pass or shoot until you've got the ball under control

Top of the foot

The top of the foot cushion is the most difficult technique. It employs a small area of the foot and the potential for miscontrolling the ball is great. The top of the foot is best used to control a dropping ball and, when mastered, this skill is not only effective but also impressive.

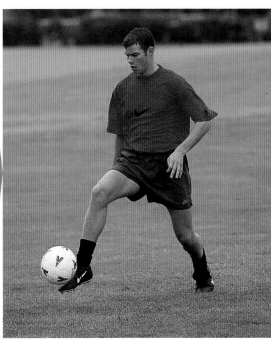

● Position your foot as early as you can and watch the ball onto the top of your foot. As the ball arrives you should pull your foot down with the ball almost resting on top of it.

③ Head, chest and thigh control

The ability to control the ball, using different parts of the body while under pressure from markers, is vital to all players. No matter how frenetic the game, all great players have time on the ball. This is because a true first touch gives you the opportunity to assess your options and make a telling contribution.

In most games, you will only have a matter of seconds to receive, control and pass the ball to a team-mate. If your first touch is poor, the ball will squirt away and you will waste time chasing it and you may squander possession.

Once possession is lost you have to work twice as hard to retrieve the situation. There are all sorts of ways, and numerous parts of the body, with which to control the ball. You should try to master them all so that you can deal with balls at any height and angle.

Whether you are planning to use your head, chest or thigh the most important things to remember are these:
1. Keep your eyes firmly on the ball (not your opponent) as it approaches you, watching it onto the part of the body you have chosen to control it with.
2. Concentrate on getting your body into a good position to receive the ball. Balance is important, so make sure you are relaxed and not leaning too far forward
3. Make up your mind early and execute your move swiftly. Making the right decision and displaying good control will often enable you to avoid being tackled.
4. Practise.

Chest and thigh

The technique for controlling the ball either on the chest or the thigh is much the same. It is all about watching the ball and cushioning it so that it drops nicely to your feet. When using the chest it is important to be in a good body position, on your toes and leaning back slightly as the ball makes contact with you. When the ball hits your chest it will begin to drop and you will be in position to complete the control with your feet.

When controlling the ball with the thigh remember to watch the ball until contact is made. Your thigh should be positioned at an angle of 45 degrees to the ground. Once again, cushion the ball and, as you bring your leg down, the ball will drop to your feet.

Head

Using your head to control a high ball is more difficult. Being relaxed and well balanced is essential in this case. The aim is to cushion the ball with the front part of your forehead. Remember, you are not looking to head the ball any great distance so, as with the chest control, you should be leaning back slightly, watching the ball onto your forehead and guiding it back to the ground. You will then need to adjust your body position quickly to enable you to control the ball with your feet before moving on.

In addition to using your feet, there are three other parts of the body which can be used to control a moving ball. The head, chest and thigh can be used to cushion the ball and take the weight out of a high pass. You are not always going to receive a pass along the ground, so it is important to know how to deal with a high ball and bring it to rest before an opponent has time to close you down.

● To control the ball on your chest, you must get into position as early as you can and watch the ball onto the large area of your chest. Lean back and direct the ball into your stride.

● Thigh control is rarely used but it is a technique worth mastering. The key is to cushion the ball and pull it downwards, rather than push it up and away from your body.

● Dribbling through cones is one of the best ways to perfect your skills. Concentrate on turning with the ball – to be truly effective, you must be able to turn both ways, otherwise you will become predictable.

A time to dribble and a time to pass

When you receive the ball you must usually decide what to do very quickly. The most frequent choice to be made, is whether to pass to a team-mate or take on an opponent. There is no time for indecision or the moment will be lost.

The important thing is knowing when and in which areas of the field to take up the dribbling option. Don't, for example, try and beat two or three opponents on the edge of your own penalty area – not unless you fancy a dressing-down from a stressed-out coach. The final third of the field is the best area to show off your skills and turn on the style with a mazy dribble.

Tricks of the trade

One-versus-one situations can be cat and mouse affairs, especially in the classic confrontations between wingers and full-backs. All the great dribblers have a vast repertoire of skills and tricks which they use to bewitch opponents. The step-over, the drag back, the scissors and many other exciting moves are the standard fare of top wingers. All of these skills should only be used once you have mastered the most effective and widely used dribbling technique: the body swerve. This move is simple in theory – you merely feint to go one way and then check back and take the ball in the opposite direction – but it takes a great deal of practice to perfect. The key to the body swerve is to make the feint (or dummy) seem convincing.

● The defender has put the attacker in a difficult position as he has successfully closed down the space. The attacker feints to go to his left, by dropping his left shoulder as shown.

● The defender is now committed to going to the attacker's left and as he does so, the forward dramatically changes direction, going back to the right and taking the ball with the outside of his right foot.

Football is a team game but there is still plenty of room for individual skill to flourish. Let's face it, one of the great sights in football is that of a skilful player on a mazy, jinking run, taking on and beating defender after defender. Dribbling with the ball, at speed, is a wonderful art. It is also an art which is all too rarely seen in the modern game, where so much emphasis is placed on team play. Nevertheless, dribbling is a potentially lethal part of a player's armoury.

Practice

Dribbling is very much an individual skill, so it's difficult to teach. But, by practising with a ball and a few cones you can develop your control and your own dribbling style. When practising, bear in mind a few key principles:

1. Make sure you have the ball under control before you begin your run, and keep it there throughout.
2. Keep the ball close to your feet. Good dribblers seem to have the ball tied to their boots, making it very difficult for opponents to win it.
3. Keep your eye on the ball...
4. ...but it is also important to keep looking up and continually checking your options.
5. Be confident.

● From the crouched position shown, the attacker knocks the ball away from his opponent (not too far) and sprints away from him. By the time the defender has recovered his balance, the attacker will be past him.

Pass masters

The greatest passers in modern football have been as happy to use a short side-foot pass as a glorious 50-yard, high, bending pass. The side-foot is the most effective way of making sure your pass arrives at a team-mate's feet. There are three elements to a good pass: accuracy, weighting and timing.

ACCURACY is the most important aspect of passing because, without it, a move breaks down and your team loses possession. Your team-mates – and your coach – will appreciate you more if you can deliver the ball accurately. Don't try anything too ambitious, just make sure you retain possession – pass to a team-mate not an opponent.

WEIGHTING, i.e. the strength or speed of a pass, is critical. It's no good hitting an accurate ball to a colleague if there's too much pace on the pass. It will be difficult to control and is likely to result in possession being squandered. Similarly, if the pass is too weak, the likelihood is that it will be intercepted before it reaches its intended target.

TIMING, the art of knowing when to release the ball, is all down to good judgement and is something only experience and practice can perfect.

If you combine these three elements with vision and perception, you will be an asset to any team.

● **Side-foot passing uses the largest area of the side of the foot. Position your non-kicking foot next to the ball and strike through the ball. The follow-through will help dictate the weight of the pass.**

The lifeblood of a football team is the art of good passing. In a nutshell, good passing is knowing where and when to hit the ball, with accuracy and the right weight. There are many types of pass, but the most important is the 'side-foot' pass. This pass is the most reliable way of shifting the ball from one player to another. The kicking foot is turned out at right angles to the direction of the pass, thus securing a good contact with the largest available area of the foot. Such passes are invariably used over short distances and offer a high level of both control and accuracy.

● Take time to practise your passing. Kicking a ball against a wall will help you to develop not only your passing, but also your control.

● A passing circle is another excellent way to hone your skills. Accuracy is everything, if your pass is badly directed or poorly weighted it will fail to make its intended target.

Tips

● Stand upright and relax as you strike the ball
● If you are trying to hit a pass along the ground, do not lean back
● Use the large area on the inside of the foot
● Concentrate on the pace of the pass – a sloppy ball will play a team-mate into trouble
● Don't switch off once you've made your pass. Run into position for a return ball. Pass and move, don't just stand and admire what you've done

6 Tackling

A skill for all

Many people take tackling for granted, but it is a genuine skill and needs to be practised. A good tackler will win the ball cleanly and will rarely give away a free-kick. A poor tackler will impatiently lunge in – often missing the ball or, more likely, catching both ball and opponent. Diving- or sliding-in is a waste of energy and can give away dangerous free-kicks and penalties or lead to injuries.

A well-timed tackle, like a goal, can be the difference between a victory and a defeat. A last-ditch challenge, made cleanly and clinically on the six-yard line, can avert a certain goal while a poor, ill-timed tackle can result in a penalty and a goal for the opposition. It is important, therefore, that every player in the team – even the goalkeeper – knows how to tackle. It is not just a defender's skill.

The art of tackling

The art of tackling is to win the ball cleanly and either come away with it in your possession, or put it out of play and out of danger. It has nothing to do with wild lunging challenges or harming opponents. Timing is central to good tackling; you must know when to make your attempt to win the ball. Don't commit yourself to the tackle too soon or you could be left on your backside and out of the game. Consider the position of your fellow defenders; committing yourself when you are the last man can be disastrous. Instead of lunging in, you should try and hold your opponent up and wait for team-mates to get back. In all cases, you should 'jockey' (hold up) your opponent until you feel the moment is right to pounce. Only make your tackle when you think you have a good chance of coming away with the ball. But when you have made up your mind to tackle, you must be decisive. Make a solid challenge and make it count. Half-hearted tackles not only give your opponent a better chance of keeping possession, but can also result in injury.

The slide tackle

The slide tackle is the most dramatic way of winning the ball, but it requires perfect timing and if it goes wrong can be dangerous. It is not an option for the inexpert, as it frequently results in the opponent being brought down, and if the ball isn't won a free-kick is conceded – maybe even a booking if the tackle is from behind. However, the slide tackle can be devastating, particularly when executed by forwards who can often win the ball in attacking areas from surprised defenders. The key is to keep pace with the opponent and slide in when he least expects it, nicking the ball from him before you nick him and bring him down. Try to make the tackle so that you are on your feet and away with the ball before the opponent has a chance to recover.

The block tackle

The most common tackle in football is the 'block tackle'. This is when two opposing players arrive for the same ball at the same time. When you reach this 50-50 situation it is vital that you don't 'pull-out' of the challenge at the last minute. This can result in injury. Meet your opponent with a strong tackle, getting your body weight over the top of the ball to add to the strength of your challenge. Good body position and a bit of determination ensure that it doesn't always have to be the bigger, stronger player who emerges with the ball.

If you don't have possession of the ball, you are not going to score… unless, that is, you are playing against very charitable opposition with a tendency to score own goals. When you lose possession, the whole team must work to cover, close down and, most importantly, win the ball back.

● The player in red pursues her opponent but is not yet in a position to tackle.

● Having caught up with the blue player, the red-shirted defender is able to slide across her opponent and strike the ball.

● The tackle is successful and the ball is won cleanly. Note that the challenge is made with studs facing away from the opponent and the tackling foot on the ground.

● To win a block tackle you must get more of your foot on the ball than your opponent. Make a firm, but controlled, contact and push the ball over the top of your opponent's foot.

Closing down

Work as a team

Whenever possession is lost, the immediate priority is to win the ball back which means getting yourself into a position to make a tackle or a block. Closing down is the first stage on the way to winning the ball back. To be effective the whole team must work together and force an error out of the opposition – this might be a poor pass, which is intercepted, or poor control, which gives the opportunity to tackle.

An opponent who has received, or is receiving, the ball should be put under immediate pressure. He must be allowed neither space nor time to bring the ball under control. However, at the same time, you must not dive in. Try to hold your opponent up and, if you can, channel him to run with the ball on his weaker side. By doing this, you may bring about a piece of poor control and a tackling opportunity.

● The player in red has the ball in the right full-back position but is closed down quickly by the blue attacker.

● The blue attacker greets her opponent, who is now boxed in to a corner, with a strong block tackle.

● Having won the block tackle, the blue attacker now has the ball in a dangerous position on the wing.

Tips

● Be aware of all opponents, and not just the player in possession
● If you are not in a position to tackle, close down the space
● Stay on your feet and do not commit yourself to a challenge that you will struggle to make
● Encourage team-mates, especially when they are looking tired
● Don't go so tight to an opponent that you make it easy for them to 'roll' you and turn you
● Defend from the front and defend as a team

Closing down an opponent who has the ball will deny that player time and space, thereby restricting his options and forcing an error. However, for closing down to be effective, you have to make sure that the whole team is covering and marking all of your opponents. If the player being closed down has one easy outlet, your hard work will be in vain.

● The blue team have possession, but as soon as the player on the edge of the box receives the ball he is closed down. The red player shepherds his opponent towards the wing and blocks his route to goal.

A worthwhile task

Closing down and tracking are tasks that appear unglamorous, but this type of hard work is highly valued by players, coaches and managers. All the best players work hard for their team and make efforts to win possession back when the ball is lost.

Top tip

● When closing down an opponent you should move toward the ball with a side-on stance. If you stand square-on, with your legs wide apart, you're likely to fall victim to an embarrassing nutmeg.

Short or tall, head the ball

Heading is one of the most neglected skills in football. It is also an extremely valuable skill. A player who is strong in the air is an asset to any team, but a player who can't head a ball, no matter how good he is on the ground, will never make the most of his ability. Only in five-a-side is the ball played exclusively along the ground, during a typical 11-a-side game the ball will be airborne for 30 per cent of the time it's in play. If you can't compete when the ball's not on the deck, you're a passenger to your team. But don't despair, anyone can learn to head the ball. It's a technique that requires practice and a little courage at first!

You don't have to be a giant centre-forward or centre-back to be a good header of the ball. Of course, there are times when being tall makes the difference between winning and losing an aerial challenge. But there's more to the art of heading than just being tall. Some shorter players are excellent headers of the ball. By the same token some tall players find it hard to win aerial challenges. Positioning and timing are just as important as a few extra inches of standing height.

Top tip

● A good way to improve your heading, and boost your confidence, is to practise jumping and heading a suspended ball. Also see how many times you can head a ball against a wall without it touching the floor.

● Get into position as early as you can, watch the ball onto your forehead and bring your neck forward as you make contact.

Heading the old fashioned heavy footballs with their hard laces was a dangerous business, but nowadays the modern ball poses no such threat. There is no good reason to avoid an aerial challenge... it's just a matter of confidence. Beat the fear and get your head on the ball.

The art of heading

The skill of heading sounds simple enough, but it is quite a complex art and many players, even top pros, fail to master it. The key to heading is making sure that the forehead is the point of contact. A common mistake is to use the top of the head. A mistake that many players, especially young ones, make is to close their eyes just before the moment of contact. Even some pros are guilty of this error. The proper way to head a ball is to get into position beneath the ball as early as possible, and to watch it onto your head. It is critical to keep your eyes open if you are going to make a good contact and give yourself the best possible chance of directing the header towards goal or a team-mate.

The neck muscles also come into play. Tense them as you bring your head back before 'attacking' the ball with power. Get the technique right and you will be surprised how much power and pace you can generate from a header. Also concentrate on judging the flight of the ball be aware of who is around you and use your whole body to elevate yourself.

Confidence

For all players, the most important thing to conquer is the fear of going up for a high ball. In the past there were real dangers in heading footballs. The ball was made of thick, heavy leather and was held together by a lace. During the course of the game the ball would absorb water and become even heavier. Heading a ball like this could knock a man unconscious if he caught it wrong, and if the lace holes caught a player on the head he could be left with a nasty gash. Nowadays, footballs are coated with vinyl to protect them from the wet and have no lace holes, so the risks of getting injured by the ball when heading are minimal.

The best way to improve your heading confidence is to practise jumping and heading a suspended ball (place a ball in a carrier bag and suspend it on a rope). Once you are happy heading a ball unchallenged, you must develop your heading in practice games and matches. The important thing is to jump with purpose and be confident you are going to win the ball. Be strong and be decisive.

● Defensive headers are all about gaining height and distance. Get underneath the ball and head it upwards using your forehead.

● The golden rule when heading for goal is to head down. Time your jump to get above the ball.

Tips

● For most heading, the forehead should be used, as it provides both power and accuracy.
● Heading the ball should not hurt. So don't be afraid and always keep your eyes on the ball all the way to impact.
● Remember, it doesn't matter if you are short or tall, you can still head the ball. If you are shorter you will need to concentrate on timing your jump, judging the flight of the ball and getting a good spring at the right moment.
● Use the neck muscles and the upper body to gain power and distance. Your arms can help you gain height and will aid balance.

BALL SKiLLS 3

In the final analysis, sport is about entertainment. And, while a well-constructed passing move may get the football purists purring, there is no more entertaining sight in football than that of a skilful forward beguiling his way past an unwitting defender. Tackles may be greeted with roars, and applause may follow goals, but it is only the ball skills and trickery of a footballing wizard that can prompt supporters to gasp and shift to the edges of their seats.

In the past many coaches frowned upon their players spending time juggling a ball around the training ground. 'You're not in the circus… that will get you nowhere in a match,' came the call from the touchline. Thankfully attitudes have now changed and the benefits of players having good juggling skills are widely appreciated.

The great thing about juggling is that it is a skill that you can practise on your own in a relatively small area. Developing your 'keepy-up' technique will improve your close control, balance and confidence when dealing with balls which arrive at an awkward height. It is also good fun.

Start by working on your basic foot juggling. Drop the ball onto your foot or roll it back onto your instep and flick it up, to begin the juggle. Once the ball is in the air, try to stay relaxed – don't plant all your weight on your standing foot, otherwise you won't be able to adjust your position to keep the juggle going. Strike the ball firmly (though not so hard that you lose control) with the top of your boot. Keep your eyes on the ball at all times. When you are happy juggling the ball on your stronger foot try moving it onto your weaker foot.

● Always keep your eyes on the ball when juggling. If you lose concentration the ball is likely to spin off the wrong part of your foot. Control your strike to keep the ball at the height you want. It is also important to stay light on your feet so you can readjust if your touch is not true.

Top tip

● Watch professionals warming-up before a match. Many will juggle the ball to hone their touch ahead of kick-off.

Foot catch

Keeping a ball up in the air is a difficult skill to master, but so too is the art of catching and holding a ball on your foot. The foot catch is a great test of control and balance. In theory, the skill is very simple: juggle the ball on your foot then, as the ball comes down, position your foot beneath it and pull the ball down cushioning it between the bottom of your shin and the top of your foot. Pull your foot up toward your shin to keep the ball in place. Sounds very simple, but the margin for error is slim – if you don't get your foot in exactly the right position the ball will slide off. The only way to perfect this skill is practice and lots of it.

● The foot catch is a difficult skill to master. The art is to get your foot positioned beneath the ball as early as you can. Pull the ball down using the top of the foot and then catch it between shin and foot. Try to maintain your balance by keeping your standing leg flexed.

Thigh Juggle

Juggling is all about innovation, so when you're happy keeping the ball up with your foot try using other parts of your body. The thigh is a perfect surface for juggling as it is wide and reasonably flat. Start your juggle with your feet and, when you have the ball under control, flick the ball up to chest height. Position your thigh at right angles to your body and strike the ball as it arrives at waist height.

Individual skills

As your skills develop try to control the ball in as many different ways as you can. This will help you improvise during matches when the ball arrives awkwardly. The back of the heel is a good surface to control the ball with, as is the outside of the foot.

● As your confidence grows, try using other parts of the foot when juggling. The back of the heel is ideal. Concentrate on keeping your balance and be prepared to adjust your position if you mishit the ball.

Neck catch

If you are feeling really confident with your juggling skills, a great move to practise and perfect is the neck catch. Although this skill has no practical use in a match situation, it will teach you the importance of balance, control and keeping your eye on the ball. The key to the neck catch is to get the ball moving over your head and to duck underneath it, watching it for as long as you can. As the ball arrives over your neck you must pull it down, lifting your head up to wedge it between your neck and shoulder blades.

● Catch the ball on your foot and flick it up. As the ball moves over your head, drop your shoulders and cushion it into place.

● Lift your head to catch the ball between neck and shoulder blades.

● The ball is in place. Try to concentrate on keeping your balance.

The Ardiles flick

Flicking the ball into the air provides a golden opportunity to show your skills. Many professionals use a fancy flick to pick the ball up before taking a corner or a throw. These skills are really only for show but, though of little use in a match, they are great fun and also help hone your skills. The most popular flick is associated with former Argentina midfielder Osvaldo Ardiles, who employed the overhead flick to great acclaim in the football film *Escape to Victory*. Ardiles, who was a World Cup winner with Argentina in 1978, amazingly used this skill in a match for English team Tottenham Hotspur some years later. However, for most players this should be a 'training-ground-only' move.

● Lean forward and drag the ball up the back of your standing leg (in this case the left) using the sole of the other foot (right).

Pincer flick

To perfect the pincer flick you will need a good touch and fast feet. The ball is flicked up between both feet and, because it doesn't rise very high, you have to be very quick to get your foot back underneath the ball to control it. This skill will encourage you to react quickly and stand lightly on your feet. Pincer flicks are popular with full-backs who need to pick up the ball to take a throw-in, and it is also a neat way to start a juggle.

● Position the ball between your feet, keeping your legs flexed.

● Knock the ball with one foot onto the other.

● Lift your foot to flick the ball into the air.

● Adjust your position and get your foot back under the ball to start your juggle.

● As the ball reaches your calf take your right foot away.

● Bring your left foot up, striking the ball up and over your head. Watch the ball over and onto your foot.

The step-over

There are two types of step-over which have proved both popular and effective in the modern game. The first requires the use of just one foot and is a step over the ball from outside to in, followed by a flick away using the outside of the same foot.

The second type of step-over (illustrated here) is for players who are both confident and competent with both feet as it requires a right foot approach, followed by a left foot take away (or vice versa).

This is a tried and trusted trick for some of the world's best forwards. The move requires balance, deception and a swift change of direction. The idea is to make the defender believe that you are intending to take him on down his left-hand side, but by stepping over and round the ball from inside to out you have provided yourself with the opportunity to take the ball away with your left foot down the defender's right-hand side. The defender is thrown off balance thus giving you vital seconds in which to get away.

1. As the attacker approaches, the defender sees that he is moving the ball with the outside of his right foot. The defender assumes his opponent intends to take him on around the outside.
2. Instead of knocking the ball past the defender with the outside of his right foot, the player runs the same foot around the front of the ball in a circular motion from inside to out. Note the defender moves towards his left. The right foot is outside the ball and slightly forward of it to enable the player to bring his left foot across for the take away.
3. By quickly adjusting his feet, the attacker's right foot is now wide of the ball and his left is inside ready to knock it away with the outside of the boot.
4. The defender is committed to going to his left, but the forward has changed his direction of attack and is away from his marker.

Drag back

The drag back

The drag back is a move which most top-class attacking players have in their repertoire of tricks and skills. It is a move which is designed to tease and torment embarrassed opponents and which is both effective and entertaining. The attacking player cheekily shows the ball to his or her opponent while moving forwards. However, just as the defender thinks the ball is within reach, the attacker drags the ball back and away from the defender's lunge. The sole of the boot is used to direct the ball backwards, while the inside of the same foot guides it away from the defender and into space.

1. The attacker 'shows' the ball to his opponent as he approaches and the defender prepares to make his tackle.
2. As the defender dives in, the attacker puts his foot on the ball and prepares to drag it back towards his own body.
3. The body is perfectly balanced as the attacker rolls the ball back using the sole of his boot. Already he is preparing to use the same foot to push the ball away. The player has turned his foot square to the ball and is in position to go past the defender on the outside as his opponent's momentum continues to take him the other way.
4. The defender is committed to his tackle and the attacker is in the clear.

Football in the 1970s was all about skill and entertainment. Winning, of course, was important, but this was a decade dominated by gifted individuals and great characters, who delighted and excited football fans the world over with their unique genius.

Franz Beckenbauer, George Best, Jairzinho and Pele were all household names, but it was the Dutchman Johan Cruyff who was the real symbol of this era of 'fantasy football', a beautifully balanced player whose repertoire of skills was breathtaking.

The 'total football' approach of the Dutch national team at the time of the 1974 World Cup finals (Holland ultimately lost to West Germany in a classic final) caught the imagination of people inside and outside the sport alike.

Cruyff was Holland's captain and the team's inspiration, displaying outrageous skills and wonderful vision – all undertaken with the utmost grace and finesse; all designed to bamboozle even the smartest defenders. One of the many moves he perfected – in addition to his ability to score wonderful goals – still carries his name today... the Cruyff turn.

If you get it right, the Cruyff turn will allow you to beat a defender and open up space to move into, throwing your opponent completely out of the game in the process. Get it wrong, and you will invariably lose possession for your team – and probably fall flat on your face in doing so – which is why this move should only be used in attacking areas... not on the edge of your own penalty area.

Cruyff mastered the art and many players have done so since. Most players can only turn one way. Practise turning both ways – you'll be a nightmare for defenders to mark if you can perfect it. The key to the turn is to convince your marker that you are going to play the ball forwards to go past him on the outside. Your body position should make him think that is what you are going to do but then, at the last moment, sell him the dummy.

● The Cruyff turn is all about deception. Here the player is making the defender believe he wants to go past him on the outside and perhaps produce a cross, or shot, with his right foot (1). But instead of taking the ball on, he stops quickly in his tracks (2) and takes his right foot around the side of the ball, knocking it behind his standing foot as shown (3). Having flicked the ball inside the defender with the inside of his right foot, the player turns sharply away from his opponent, who is still committed to his forward motion (4).

Top tip

● Don't become predictable by trying to use the Cruyff turn too often in a game. Your move will become easy to read. Keep defenders guessing by using it sparingly and only when the need arises.

1

2

3

4

When an attacker runs at an opponent, his primary aim is to make the defender commit himself. If you can make your opponent gamble by convincing him that you are heading in one direction, you are halfway to tricking your way past him. Once the defender has committed himself, you will be free to move away in the opposite direction and into space.

The shimmy is one of the best methods of getting a defender to commit to a challenge. As you run at your marker, put your right foot down outside the ball and then lift your left foot as if you are about to strike the ball from left to right. This movement with your left leg is the shimmy and needs to be exaggerated. Once you have performed your shimmy you must move the ball in the opposite direction (right to left) with your right foot.

● As you run towards your opponent with the ball on your right foot fake to take the ball away with your left foot.

● Really exaggerate the movement of the left leg before taking the ball off to your left with the right foot.

The stop-start

The stop-start is a move which appears to be relatively simple, but it is in fact one that requires a deftness of touch few players are blessed with. It must be carried out while the player is in full flow and with a speed of foot that merely adds to the difficulty of the move. The stop-start is best deployed on the edge of your opponents' penalty area where a change of pace can get you past your marker and into space in the 18-yard box.

● When running with the ball prior to carrying out this skill it is important to have your eyes on the ball, not the man you are looking to beat.

● Bring your right foot up and above the ball with your standing foot close behind.

● Place your right foot down on top of the ball with a minimum of force. Do not stamp on it. Your opponent now thinks you are bringing body and ball to a halt, but with your right foot still resting gently on the ball bring your left foot forward to meet it.

● Release the pressure with the right foot and poke the ball forward with your left foot in a quick, jumping movement. The stop-start manoeuvre will confuse the defender and give you an extra yard of space.

⑥ Nutmeg

One of the most embarrassing things to happen to a player on the field – outside scoring an own goal or missing an open one – is falling victim to the dreaded nutmeg. For the player 'nutting' an opponent (the art of pushing the ball through his or her legs and gleefully running around to collect the ball the other side) the feeling of satisfaction when it comes off is almost as great as scoring a goal. For the open-stanced, red-faced opponent it is a nightmare which will continue long after the game has finished as even close pals take great delight in reminding the victim of the incident.

The simple answer, of course, is to keep your legs shut when an opponent is running toward you. In reality, it's not as easy as that. For starters, if your legs are together you are not well balanced and, worse still, not well positioned to push off in one direction or another. Keep your legs open, but not to the extent of inviting the player to take advantage with 'a meg'.

For the player in possession there are, invariably, better options available than the gamble of losing possession by trying to poke the ball through an opponent's legs. More nutmegs fail than succeed. But to many players it's an irresistible challenge and the rewards are immense.

Top tip

● Throughout the move it is important to smile at all times and, remember, no nutmeg is complete without the customary cry of 'NUTS' as you round the embarrassed opponent to collect the ball.

1. As the player in possession approaches the defender he quickly recognises the opportunity to nutmeg his open-legged opponent.
2. Decide what are you are going to do and choose the right moment to carry out the move.
3. When you consider the gap between your opponents legs to be wide enough to get the ball successfully through, go for it!
4. As soon as you've knocked the ball through his legs (not with any great force, mind) run round him to collect it. If your opponent is moving to the left you go to the right, and vice versa.

Rolling foot over ball

A defender who won't commit and instead stands up and waits for you to make the first move can be a difficult proposition. The best way to get past your stubborn marker is to force him to make a challenge. One of the many ways you can trick an opponent into committing to a challenge is to roll your foot over the ball. This is a simple skill but it can be effective if you get your technique right.

As you approach the defender you must try to deceive him into thinking that you are going to knock the ball past him. Draw your leg back as if to make a full contact with the ball, but slow your swing down as you bring your foot toward the ball. Instead of making a full contact with the ball, just lightly roll your foot over the top of it. The defender should now commit himself to a challenge and you will be able to change direction, moving into the space that has opened up. The stubborn marker is now rooted to the spot and is in no position to pursue you.

This skill is often employed by tricky midfielders, but it can also be used to force goalkeepers to go to ground in one-against-one situations.

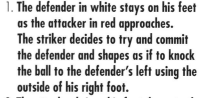

1. The defender in white stays on his feet as the attacker in red approaches.
   The striker decides to try and commit the defender and shapes as if to knock the ball to the defender's left using the outside of his right foot.
2. The attacker brings his foot down to the ball and, instead of striking it, rolls his foot over the top of the ball.
   The defender plants his left foot forward to make a challenge.
3. The attacker rolls the ball to his left and away from the, now committed, defender and moves into space.
   The defender is left rooted to the spot.

7 Round the corner

This is probably a phrase few readers have come across before, but it is a genuine name for a rarely used skill. Clever players with a subtle touch are more likely to be suited to this move than bigger, less mobile players.

Awareness of what is going on around you, especially in the space that you are hoping to run into behind your opponent, is vital. The ideal time to attempt this skill is when you have your back to goal with a defender in close attention. The opponent is probably thinking, as the pass comes into your feet, that you will hold the ball up to pass to a team-mate, or that you will try to turn with the ball in order to run at goal. What the defender will not be expecting is for you to try and beat him or her 'round the corner' in the fashion illustrated.

The Brazilian Edmundo used this technique to score a brilliant goal for Vasco de Gama against Manchester United in FIFA's inaugural World Club Championship in January, 2000.

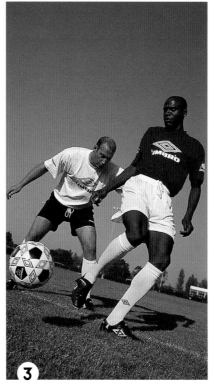

1. As the ball is played into you, be aware of the position of your opponent and the space behind which you are planning to run into.
2-3. As your opponent moves in, lean to the left and look to get the slightest of touches with the outside of your right foot. Notice how the player is looking to graze the outside of his boot down the inside of the ball.
4. If your flick is subtle enough it will cause the ball to lift gently and spin past the static defender. You begin your move around the other side of him. By twisting and turning to the left you can go round your defender with ease and collect the ball.

2

Top tip

● Playing the ball on one side of a defender and running the other is a move which is guaranteed to catch opponents on the hop. This move is similar to the 'Round the corner' in that it requires both space and subtlety. Ideally you should save this trick for use in the attacking third of the field, and when you know that you can beat your marker for pace. As you approach the defender check that you have enough space behind him to collect the ball. Try to push the ball forward at an angle so that your run will converge with its path. Measuring the forward pass is the key to this move.

PASSING 4

There is no more efficient way to get the ball forward than via an accurate pass. Entertaining dribbling skills are all very well, but if it's matches rather than applause you want to win, then take some time to master the art of passing. Start with the basics and before you know it you'll be launching 70 yard passes.

Contrary to the opinion of football purists, it is not always possible to deliver a measured and accurate pass to a team-mate. There are times during every match when you will find yourself with neither the time nor the space to pick out a colleague with a pass to feet. If you have an opponent bearing down on you, but have no team-mate within easy range, you will need an outlet. In such situations, a stock pass is called for.

A stock pass is a ball played into a predetermined area of the field, and can be used either to release pressure or to create havoc in your opponent's penalty area. The channel ball and far-post cross are two of the most commonly employed stock-passes.

● **Right: The player in red has the ball in the right-back position, but is quickly closed down by the blue forward. Rather than pump the ball into the middle of the pitch, the red player decides slides it down the channel outside the blue team's left-back. This will give the red team's forward line a chance to win the ball or force an error from the blue team's defence.**

The channel ball

A full-back who is under pressure, but who has little by way of support on the wing, has limited options. It would be risky to try and dribble the ball out from the back, as the full-back is likely to be the last line of defence on the flank. A ball played aimlessly forward is also unlikely to meet with success and will probably just come straight back at the defence. The channel ball is the solution to this problem.

Instead of aiming for a team-mate, the ball is played forward in the 'channel' between touchline and penalty area. The pass should be angled and weighted to ensure that team-mates are favourites to get to the ball ahead of their markers. Ideally the channel ball should be played in behind the opposing full-back to get the defender running back toward his, or her, own goal. Any good centre-forward will also anticipate the channel ball.

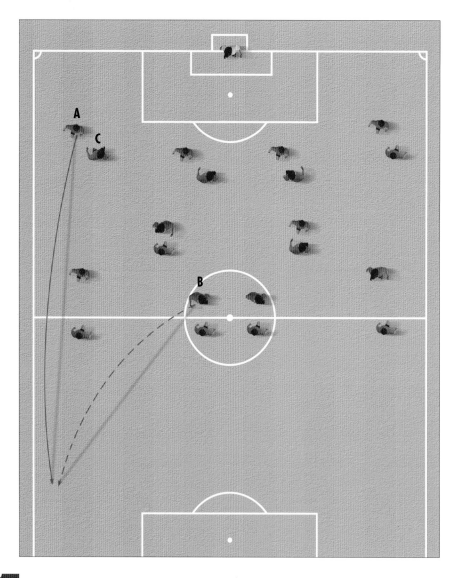

● **Player A is closed down by Player C and, with all his team-mates closely marked, elects to play a channel pass down the right wing. He pushes the ball down the line outside the full-back, leaving his team-mate (Player B) to run onto the pass.**

The far-post cross

When you have the ball on the wing in the attacking third of the field, there is usually precious little time to consider your options. Pondering for too long will often result in opportunities disappearing. On other occasions it may not be possible to measure a cross to a team-mate because of the attentions of a marker or because the ball is running perilously close to the dead-ball line. In such situations, the preferred solution is to deliver the ball into an area that will put the opposing team under maximum pressure. A far-post cross, like the channel pass, is likely to be anticipated by most strikers. It is also an extremely difficult ball to defend against.

Goalkeepers are unable to come out and catch a well-delivered far-post cross, and centre-halves have the choice of heading the ball behind for a corner or away from goal and possibly into the path of an onrushing striker.

The near-post cross

Crosses played to the near post can be just as effective as those hit to the far post. However, fewer strikers make runs to the near post as it requires a more subtle header to convert such centres.

Anticipation

The key to the success of any stock pass is anticipation on the part of team-mates. All routine passing movements should be practised in training.

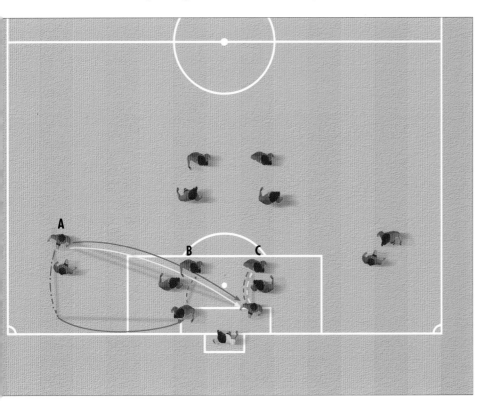

● Above: The most dangerous far-post crosses are those that bend away from the keeper. However, the key to the success of any cross lies with the receiver who must anticipate the centre. The striker here has timed her run to perfection, getting above the defender to head for goal.

● With the ball out wide on the right wing, Player A has two crossing options. Firstly, he can aim for Player B at the near-post or alternatively he can hit a longer cross to the far post where Player C is lurking. For the near-post cross to be most effective, Player A should get to the bye-line and cut the ball back toward the edge of the six-yard box. However, if he elects to play the ball in Player C's direction he is better advised to cross it early and with plenty of height.

② The swerve pass

The side-foot pass (see page 44) is the safest and one of the most effective deliveries you can make, but it is not always an option. Sometimes it is impossible to find a team-mate with a direct pass along the ground. One solution may be the swerve pass. The art of bending or curling the ball around obstacles is a favoured skill of full-backs. The swerve pass is commonly used by full-backs wanting to avoid an opponent standing in front of them as they pass to a winger standing further along the touch-line.

There are two types of swerve pass – one hit with the inside of the boot which, for a right-footed player, will arc the ball from right to left, and the other with the outside of the boot which, again taking the example of a right-footer, will curl from left to right. The margin for error when hitting a pass with the inside of the foot is less than that which applies to striking a ball with the outside. Either way, both skills require much practice.

● **The key to bending the ball is to strike across it and follow through with your striking leg. Only attempt to bend the ball round an opponent when you're confident in your ability. Practise bending the ball round a team-mate until you have mastered the skill.**

Tips

1. When striking the ball with the inside of the foot, 'graze' the ball rather than strike right through it.
2. The worst thing you can do is under-hit the pass and not even get the ball around your opponent. Strike the ball cleanly and with confidence.
3. In order to get the maximum amount of bend on the ball, exaggerate your follow-through.
4. Remember that passing is not just about finding a team-mate but presenting him with a ball he can control comfortably and then use effectively.

The chip pass

The chip pass is more ambitious than the swerve pass, with the margin for error even greater. However, when performed correctly it can be extremely rewarding. Failure to gain enough height on the pass results in an embarrassing pass to an opponent, so it is vital to practise this skill and have plenty of confidence before trying it in a match.

The chip can be used in all areas of the field and when used well it is extremely productive. In defence it can be used to clear an opponent who is charging in to challenge; in midfield it can be used when closed down; and in attack it is employed when a delicate chip over a defender plays a team-mate in on goal.

The correct way to play a chip is to make a 'stab' at the ball and get your foot right underneath it. Contact is made with the lower part of the instep, not the toe of the boot, and the idea is to bring the striking foot down sharply and stop quickly – this will create backspin on the ball, which should then loft the ball upwards into the air. The chip needs only a short back lift and, unlike the swerve pass, little or nothing by way of follow-through. The aim is to get enough height on the ball to clear the opponent nearest to you, so your judgement of distance is as critical as is your technique.

● **To chip the ball get your foot right underneath it and lean back. This will put backspin on the ball lofting it into the air. Like bending the ball, chipping is a difficult skill to master and one worth practising with team-mates before attempting in a match situation.**

The chest pass is a skill usually associated with strikers. It requires not only upper-body strength but also the know-how and awareness to bring a team-mate into play with an accurate, controlled pass under the severest physical pressure. Some strikers become so good at this skill that they will leap to redirect a high ball with their chest rather than their head. When perfected, the chest pass enables a player to move the ball on first time rather than slow the play down by first controlling the ball on the chest and then looking to pass to a team-mate, or turn towards goal. This skill is ideal for a ball arriving at medium height, which can be sent accurately towards the feet of a nearby colleague.

● Keep your eyes firmly on the ball and also keep yourself between your opponent and the ball at all times. Hold your arms out to present a wider target.

● Try and anticipate the trajectory of the ball and position your body accordingly.

Heading is not just for big, bruising centre-backs with the power to deliver 30-yard headed clearances, or for agile strikers who leap like salmon and score bullet headers. Heading can also be a subtle art employed by players of any size or stature.

Whatever position you play, at some time during the course of 90 minutes the ball will arrive at head-height. On most occasions your options will be simple – try to bring the ball under your control, or send a controlled, headed pass to a team-mate nearby. Trying to bring the ball under control with your head is a difficult skill and is made harder if you are under pressure from opponents, so in most situations your best option is to try to head a pass to a team-mate.

As with any form of heading, the forehead is the most logical part to use. The surface is bigger and flatter and gives you a good chance of controlling, or cushioning the ball so that it doesn't fly off at all angles. Of course, there will be times when you are looking to flick the ball to left or right, or behind you for a team-mate to run on to. In such cases the side or the top of the head are the best surfaces to use.

● The striker on the right of this picture has 'no angle' to head for goal.

Tips

1. Always keep your eyes on the ball until you have delivered your pass.
2. Make up your mind where you are going to head the ball, and to whom, and position your head and body ready to direct the pass.
3. Balance is all-important, as is the ability to control the pace of the ball.
4. Unlike defensive headers or goal attempts, the headed pass needs to be cushioned so the neck and shoulder muscles should be relaxed.
5. Allow the ball to come on to the forehead rather than meeting it with power. Remember, the direction of your header is essential.

● As the ball approaches, bend your knees, lean back and open up your chest ready to receive the pass, watching the ball all the time.

●Thrust your chest at the ball to make sure your pass reaches a team-mate and is not intercepted.

● The ball falls nicely for an on-coming colleague who is suddenly presented with a goal-scoring opportunity.

● He gets up early and directs his header back toward a team-mate.

● The ball is sent down to the feet of the oncoming player who is able to strike for goal.

The backheel pass

The backheel is the original 'fancy dan' trick. However, backheelers are not just extravagances for flashy wingers and strikers, they can also be extremely constructive if employed with both skill and caution. The backheel is particularly useful for switching the angle of an attack. With the correct technique, the back of the heel can be used to deliver passes either square (to the side) or directly behind.

A direct running forward will often find a player blocking his path but, with a square pass to a colleague in space, he can take his opponent out of the play. Using the heel to deliver a square pass can be effective as it is more difficult for a defender to read and predict.

A conventional backheel uses a similar technique to the square backheel which can be used when a player finds his path blocked by an opponent. A backheel to a team-mate just behind takes the pressure off and helps your team retain possession. Always take a look before delivery, making sure a team-mate is close enough and not tightly marked. In the modern game the backheel is employed in all areas of play – from defence to attack – though it remains a popular skill for midfielders.

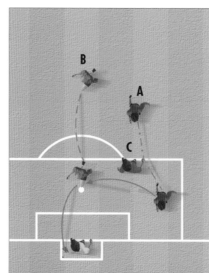

● Player A has his route to goal blocked by Player C and is forced to head out wide. However, just when it seems the blue defender has averted the danger, Player A sends a back-heel into the path of his team-mate, Player B, who is able to shoot for goal.

1-2. The attacker's route to goal is blocked by the defender and he has to move across the edge of the 18-yard box.
3. The attacker plays a back-heel pass and keeps his marker at bay by striking the ball with his right foot.
4-5. The ball is played into the path of the on-rushing red player who has a goalscoring opportunity.

The scissors pass

A well-executed scissors pass can be a devasting move for the opposition's defence to deal with. With good vision, a deft flick and quick feet you can set-up a team-mate, leave your marker standing and make yourself available for a return pass.

This may sound a complicated move, but it is not, providing you follow some basic rules:

1. Face the direction of the pass with your back to the defender marking you.
2. Bend your knees and position your striking foot (in this case the right foot slightly behind your standing foot.
3. Just before the pass arrives make a small, one-footed jump off your standing foot, lifting the playing foot ready to flick the ball behind the standing foot.
4. Strike the ball with the largest area on the inside of the boot. Control the strike and never try to hit the ball too hard — you are likely to miss it completely.

At the end of the pass your legs should be slightly crossed, hence the name the scissors pass. Good timing, and speed, are critical to this move and deceiving your opponent. Try to disguise the move so that your opponent believes you are intending to control the ball and turn, rather than flick it to an opponent to run on to. When carried out on the edge of the opposition penalty area, this can often lead to a goalscoring chance.

There are many ways to beat an opponent who stands between you and goal. One of the most simple and effective methods is the wall pass (also called a 'one-two' or a 'give and go'). If carried out correctly this technique takes you past your opponent without the need for any dribbling or trickery. It relies, instead, on a team-mate reading your intentions and reacting quickly.

In indoor five-a-side football a wall pass can be exactly that – a pass against the wall and around an opponent. The same principle applies in games played on open football pitches. The only difference is that you require a team-mate to act as 'the wall' to enable you to beat your man. This tactic is most effective when a midfield player passes the ball into a central striker on the edge of the box and continues his run to receive the ball beyond the striker.

Athletic, attacking midfielders are the best exponents of this skill. These players run from deep positions and, unless their markers are willing to track all the way back and forward with them, they create chances.

4

5

Tips

1. Your 'wall', the person you are passing to, must know what you are planning to do. Develop an understanding on the training field and practise the move.
2. For a good return pass from your colleague, you must give him a cleanly hit, accurate pass in the first place.
3. Defenders won't stand back and admire your move, they will be after you. So you must be quick off the mark after playing the ball to catch them out.
4. Make sure the ball is played wide enough to prevent the defender sticking out a leg to block the pass.

1. The player on the right has been closed down by the defender in white.
2-3. The attacker opts to pass the ball into the feet of his team-mate who, with his back to goal, holds off his marker and prepares to play a return pass.
4. The ball is played first time in behind the defender.
5. The first attacker runs onto the pass and shoots at goal.

You may not be blessed with the agility and looseness of limb to carry out that most extreme of disguised passes – the reverse pass – but with practice anybody can perfect a simple disguised pass. This skill is particularly useful when running with the ball, closely guarded by a vigilant opponent, and without a team-mate in easy passing range. You appear to be running further and further into trouble, and you're probably running out of space too. In most cases players will try to change direction, but your marker will be expecting this. The alternative is to cut the ball back in the opposite direction from that which you are running and into the path of a team-mate.

To use this skill you will need good balance and the ability to change the direction of play by readjusting your body position and wrapping your foot around the ball in order to make the pass. Smaller players with fleet of foot seem able to twist, turn and release reverse passes from dead-end runs which were going nowhere. The key to this technique, however, is an understanding of the runs your team-mates will make and an awareness of what is going on around you.

1. The player in red appears to be going nowhere as his opponent closes down his space, preventing him going wider or further upfield.
2. Hearing a shout from a team-mate, he prepares to take his only route out of trouble. However, he does not show any sign that he plans to cut the ball back.
3. He begins to adjust his body position, with his standing foot directly behind the ball. His eyes remain on the ball and not the opponent or his team-mate.
4. By wrapping his striking foot around the ball and bringing the leg around at a sharp angle he is now in a better position to whip the ball back to his team-mate.
5. With a sideways, jabbing movement the player brings his striking leg down sharply to direct a pass away from the defender with the inside of the foot.
6. The pass is perfect and suddenly the defender, having looked favourite to win the ball, is caught out.

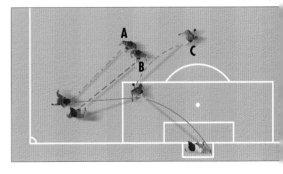

● Player A has the ball and is heading toward goal, however his path is blocked by Player B who diverts him out wide. Player A seems to be heading away from trouble but, seeing the run of his team-mate Player C, he cuts the ball back into the danger zone using a reverse pass. Player C is now in a goalscoring position.

FiNiSHiNG 5

There is no better feeling in football than the adreneline rush of scoring a goal.
Putting the ball in the net is the hardest but most rewarding aspect of the game, and if you can
master this crucial art you will find yourself not only in demand but also in the headlines.

① Placement versus power

When the ball arrives at your feet in the opposition penalty area, the one commodity you are likely to be short of is time. In such situations, hesitancy can prove costly. To avoid the frustration of having the ball taken off your toe by a quick-thinking defender you must be decisive. All good goalscorers know what they are going to do before the ball arrives and, once they have a plan they stick to it.

The fundamental decision faced by an attacker with the goal at his or her mercy is whether to go for power or placement. Each approach has its pros and cons, and while some players tend to favour one method over the other, the best strikers make their decision based on the circumstances at hand.

Hit it hard?

A shot hit powerfully toward goal is guaranteed to create havoc... unless of course you get underneath the ball and send it soaring over the bar.

Presuming that you avoid an embarrassing shot into the sky, a driven strike has several benefits. Firstly, the harder the shot the more difficult it is for the keeper to pull off a save, and even if he gets a touch on the ball, it will take a strong hand to divert it away from goal. In addition, if a powerful shot strikes a defender or keeper en route to goal, it may end up deflected into a team-mate's path. A shot driven toward goal is also unlikely to be controlled and cleared by an opponent, so at the very least you can expect to regain possession from a hurried clearance.

Technique – Power

To hit a low, hard shot you must strike the ball with your instep. Place your non-striking foot alongside the ball with your toes pointing toward goal. Fix your eyes on the ball and, keeping your head and shoulders over it, strike through the ball with the centre of your instep. Try to keep your knee over the ball at impact to keep the shot low.

● The red team's number seven has possession of the ball in the penalty area and bears down on goal.

● With a defender rapidly closing her down, the red attacker elects to drive the ball hard inside the keeper's near post.

● Although the shot ends up near the keeper, she is beaten by the pace on the shot and has no chance.

Going for accuracy

Shooting for an unguarded corner of the net requires a cool nerve and a good deal of confidence. When a placed shot finds its intended target the scorer looks every inch a top international striker, but when the shot is scuffed wide or too near the keeper, the culprit feels nothing but embarrassment. The most commonly made error is to 'quit' on the shot, so make sure that you strike the ball with purpose. The side of the foot is best for this type of shot, although the instep can also be used. Once you have made your decision all you need to do is take aim and pass the ball into the net.

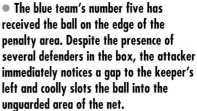

● The blue team's number five has received the ball on the edge of the penalty area. Despite the presence of several defenders in the box, the attacker immediately notices a gap to the keeper's left and coolly slots the ball into the unguarded area of the net.

Choose power...

... when the ball may get held up in a muddy penalty area
... when you don't have a clear sight of goal
... when you are being closed down by an opponent and have no time to pick your spot

Choose placement...

... when the keeper has left a large chunk of his goal unguarded
... when the keeper is coming off his line
... when an unexpected gap appears in a crowded penalty area

The volley

2

The volley is a precise skill which, when mastered, can produce explosive and spectacular results. However, there is no margin for error when trying to strike the ball while it is in the air and if you get it wrong the results can be embarrassing. Timing, co-ordination, balance and body position are all essential to this difficult skill.

The spectacular volley has been the trademark of some of the game's top players, including such luminaries as Frenchman Eric Cantona and Dutchman Marco Van Basten. And, although both Cantona and Van Basten were gifted footballers who possessed almost flawless technique, they would be the first to admit that they still needed to practise to hone their skill. At Manchester United Cantona was invariably the first and last man on the training ground and the Frenchman spent a great deal of his time perfecting the art of volleying. If players of the stature of Cantona and Van Basten feel the need to practise, the rest of us must work even harder. Practise hard and practise often if you wish to improve your volleying.

● **The ball is approaching from the player's left. He takes up his position to meet the trajectory of the ball, arms outstretched for balance.**

● **The player's eyes are permanently fixed on the ball, not the goal, and his head is over the ball in order to keep the shot down.**

Shaping up

When contemplating a volley one of the most important considerations, strange though it may seem, is the position of the non-striking foot. At the time of impact you are standing on one foot only and the power you can get into the shot will depend on how well you have positioned yourself. To get maximum power in your shot you must bring the upper part of the striking foot into contact with the moving ball. Keep your eye firmly on the ball. Unlike bending the ball, the follow-through with a volley is not that long, although it is important to remember to keep the swing of your leg smooth and not to snatch at the ball.

Top tip

● As with a golf shot, power can be generated by the timing of your strike rather than the amount of force you put into it.

● Using the front of the boot, the player strikes the ball with the 'sweet spot' to gain maximum power.

● The benefit of keeping your head over the ball is shown in this picture as the player follows through rather than stabs at the ball.

Overhead kick

There's no more exhilarating sight in football than an athletic player scoring with an acrobatic overhead kick. Such moments of improvisation are rare and are guaranteed to bring even the most conservative fans to their feet in appreciation.

Few, if any, players in recent years have scored so many goals in this unorthodox fashion as Mexican Hugo Sanchez. The former Real Madrid idol was not the tallest of strikers yet was able to launch himself to incredible heights to produce a plethora of incredible goals. The celebrations which always followed – an acrobatic somersault and back flip – also became one of his elaborate trademarks. The overhead kick is quite probably the most difficult skill in football. It requires not only a perfect technique but also a high degree of agility to reach the ball in the first place. Courage is needed too, for only a brave player would fling himself skyward to win the ball in this fashion.

Warning

Overhead kicks can be extremely dangerous to the kicker. Never use this skill on hard surfaces such as concrete or astro turf. If possible, practise using a soft crash mat to cushion your fall.

1. The leap is initiated by the non-kicking foot and you can see how the player is already beginning to lean away from the ball. Note the position of the arms.
2. The non-kicking leg is now up to waist height while the kicking foot remains on the ground. Again the arms are positioned to provide balance while the back is arched further.
3. With the body almost parallel to the ground the kicking leg now swings into action, arcing towards the ball. Note how the player's eyes have never once left the ball. The kick is completed when the kicking leg makes contact with the ball which is propelled over the head towards goal. The arms are now brought down to help cushion the fall to ground.

The scissors kick

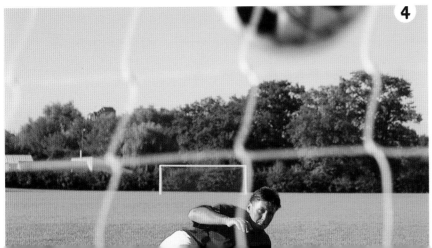

This skill is similar in many ways to that of the overhead kick. It is used to strike balls played at between knee and shoulder height and gets its name because the legs cross quickly, as the player is in mid-air, in a scissors motion. The ball is struck on the volley and, like the overhead kick, this skill requires both a high level of technical ability as well as athleticism.

1. The player is side-on to the goal and facing the cross, which is coming towards him from the right wing. The left arm is already out for balance and the player is on his toes ready to leap into action.
2. Leaning back slightly and with arms outstretched the player now assesses the height of the cross and the kicking leg is pulled back ready for the strike.
3. As contact is made with the ball the non-kicking leg leaves the ground and the player is airborne as the kicking foot swings round to face the goal.
4. By spinning round in the air the player's body now faces the goal.

Top tip

● Attempting to kick the ball when it is at head height or above can be deemed dangerous play if opponents are close, so awareness of their position is vital.

The chip and the scoop

A delicate chip over a six-foot keeper is a dream for a striker; a nightmare for any goalie.

Timing is at the essence of lobbing or chipping a keeper. If you delay your effort for too long the keeper will get back in time to catch the ball as it tamely drops goalward. So weigh up your options and if the lob is on, with the keeper off his line, take your chance. Without awareness and vision you will never be able to perfect this skill.

Basic technique

To get the ball into the air, you will need to strike underneath it using a stabbing motion. Lean back as you strike the ball and don't follow through. Practise so that you are able to vary the height and distance of the lob.

1. The player prepares to chip the ball using the instep having spotted the keeper off his line.
2. Like a golfer with a lofted club, he chips the ball goalwards using a stabbing motion in order to gain instant height.
3. The player's strike is perfect and has enough height and weight to carry over the stranded goalkeeper. Concentrate on getting the right amount of pace and height on the ball so that it clears the keeper and also drops beneath the crossbar into an empty net.

The scoop

Only a player with supreme confidence, and more than a touch of arrogance, would attempt this particular form of finishing. There are more conventional ways of beating a keeper in a 'one-against-one' situation, but this is a guaranteed crowd pleaser... if it comes off, that is!

Goals scored as a result of 'the scoop' are few and far between. However football fans were treated to the most audacious of scoops in the quarter-finals of the European Championships in 1996. In a game of few chances, the Czech Republic winger Karel Poborsky caught the Portugal keeper Vitor Baia completely by surprise as he flicked the ball over him and into the net from the edge of the 18-yard box. Poborsky's goal was all the more notable as he scooped a moving ball while running toward goal – most players would only attempt this difficult skill from a static position.

1. **As the keeper comes off his line, the striker positions his standing foot beside the ball and prepares to scoop the ball.**
2. **Leaning back as he strikes the ball, the player makes a full follow-through while maintaining his balance.**
3. **Clearing the keeper is one thing, but the scoop needs to be controlled for the ball to drop under the bar.**
   Practise this skill on the training ground, varying your follow-through to change the pace and height of your scoops.

To scoop or to chip

The scoop and the chip have the same aim – to get the ball over a keeper who is off his line and down quickly enough to fall under the bar and into the net. The chip can be used when shooting from as far out as the halfway line, but it is difficult to get the ball to come down quickly enough when you are in the 18-yard box. From close in on goal the scoop is a more useful skill as it is possible to loop the ball over a standing keeper from inside the penalty area. Both of these techniques require a high level of skill and therefore a great deal of practice.

Top tip

● Check the positioning of the keeper early on in the game. If he likes to stray to the edge of his 18-yard box when the ball is in the midfield you may be able to lob him.

5

Merest of touches

The glancing header

In most cases the forehead is used to head the ball. After all, it is the flattest part of the head and when the connection with the ball is good it generates power and provides a better chance of accuracy. But power is not the main issue with the glancing header, although accuracy is obviously a priority. The margin for error with this type of header is much greater. A run to the near post and a weak attempt at a glancing header is an all too common sight. Either the player fails to make enough contact between the side of the head and the inside of the ball, or he gets too much on the ball and meets it full on, sending the ball back in the direction from which it came.

The key to this skill is making the right contact with the right part of the head on the right section of the ball. When you get all three things correct you have a better than even chance of getting your header on target. To score a goal, the contact needs to be true in order to guide the ball away from the keeper — as the pictures show.

Tips

1. **Time your run, so that you arrive with the ball at a comfortable height to head.**
2. **Keep your eye on the ball rather than the goal.**
3. **Try to run across the ball so that you can easily meet it with the side of your head.**
4. **Twist your neck as you make contact to steer the ball goalwards.**

● You can see the player is going to have to head the ball at an angle of 120 degrees to the cross in order to stand a chance of beating the keeper.

● He does this by glancing the ball with the side of the head and helping the ball goalwards with a twist of the neck.

Smashing the ball home with enough force to break the net provides a tremendous feeling of invigoration, but there are occasions when a more subtle finish is called for. The two techniques demonstrated here put the emphasis on directing the ball rather than striking it, and in both cases the pace of the finish is derived from the cross. To perfect these moves takes guile rather than brute strength.

The flick finish

A cross played along the ground to the near post is a difficult ball for a striker. Such a pass does not give the recipient a simple chance for a shot, unless of course he or she has time and space to control the ball and turn. In most cases, however, this will not be possible and instead the solution lies in what we have called The flick finish . This skill utilises the basic technique used in the scissors pass (see page 77), so instead of striking the ball with your leading leg, you let it run slightly behind you before striking it with the leg which is furthest from goal. Use the inside of your boot to hit the ball, guiding it behind the other leg and toward goal. Timing is all important to this move, because if you are a fraction of a second out you will miss the ball or guide it into your standing leg. Practice is the only way to hone your sense of timing. Time spent on the training ground working on this skill will also help you to develop your ability to angle the ball into different areas of the goal.

1. The red team's winger has got to the line and prepares to deliver a cross.
2. The red's number seven has anticipated a near-post cross and gets in front of her marker.
3. As the ball arrives, she lets it run past her left foot and strikes it with the inside of her right.
4. The goalkeeper is left rooted to the spot as the ball rolls past her and into the net.

6

Heading for goal

The diving header

Not only must you possess good heading technique and agility for this skill, you must also be as brave as a lion. Diving low to head the ball in a crowded penalty area means you run the risk of getting a kick in the face.

The diving header is used when the ball arrives at between shoulder and knee height. The other option for balls played at this height is the scissors kick; however this offers less control than the header. Different situations call for different techniques, and while it may be worth diving in amongst the boots to head a winner in a World Cup final, sticking your neck out in a practice match may not be worth the risk.

Top tip

● Even though you are putting your head in amongst the flying feet and probably don't wish to see what's coming, you must keep your eyes open and firmly fixed on the ball at all times. A whack in the face is going to hurt whether you see it coming or not and, once you've committed yourself to the header, there's no way out.

1. The player is using his left leg to project himself forward towards the ball played from the wing, which is coming at below head height.
2. Both feet are in the air and the player is virtually horizontal to the ground in classic diving header style, with the forehead making powerful contact with the ball.
3. The attacker literally launches himself at the ball to gain extra power, twisting his head to direct the ball goalward and putting his arms out to protect his fall.

The far post header

There was a time, not so long ago, when the far post header was the stock-in-trade of any self-respecting number-nine. However, following the decline of the old style winger and the cross from the dead-ball line, this classic striking skill has become all too rare in the modern game.

A good far post header requires two things: timing and a quality cross. A centre-forward cannot, of course, control the delivery of the ball, but he can work on his timing and technique to ensure that he makes good use of any crosses that make it into the danger zone. Try to time your run so that you arrive at the far post in time to get ahead of your marker and meet the ball with your forehead. You will probably have to start making your run long before the ball is crossed, but it is well worth gambling because if the ball makes it past the keeper you will find yourself in a goalscoring position. Once you have made your mind up to go to the far post you must attack the ball, bracing yourself for the physical challenge that will inevitably arrive. As with all attacking headers, your prime concern should be to keep the ball down, so if possible you should try to rise above the ball.

● The blue striker attacks the ball as it arrives at the far post and, in so doing, gives herself a great advantage over the hesitant red defender.

Top tip

● Take great care to avoid inadvertently fouling your opponent when heading at the far post. Many referees will give the benefit of the doubt to the defender if you knock him or her over in your efforts to get to the ball. Keep your arms away from your opponent as much as you can and try to resist the temptation to lead with your elbow.

⑦ The swerve shot

The art of bending the ball around a wall at free-kicks is explained on page 108 and the same principles apply when attempting a curler in open play. Because you are running at speed with a defender perhaps no more than a yard away – as opposed to ten yards at a free-kick – it is logical to assume that bending a moving ball is more difficult than doing so from a dead-ball situation. However, many players are more confident striking a ball on the run and feel they can get more 'bend' on the ball than they can from a static position.

Your first thought when attempting a curling shot is the position of the goalkeeper and the point of the goal you are looking to hit. Usually, when a player is trying to bend a ball in this way, the inside of the far post is the target – although strikers often catch keepers off guard by curling the ball towards the near post. If you're attempting the former, you should be looking to aim the ball wide of the goal, hitting around the closest defender, in order to try and curl it back inside the far post but out of the keeper's reach.

In order to do this start the ball off about two to three feet (one metre) outside the post, curling the ball with the inside of the boot, bringing it from right to left if you are right-footed or from left to right if you are left-footed. It is important to hit the ball with pace, as well as spin, so that the keeper has less time to get across his goal and make a save. A fraction of a second is critical in these situations.

● By positioning your body square on to the ball and almost parallel to the goal you have a better chance of 'wrapping' your striking foot around the ball with the inside of the boot.

● To bend the ball from left to right hit across the left half of the ball rather than striking through the middle as you would normally. Set the ball wide of the goal, away from the nearest opponent.

It is not necessary to use the left foot to bend the ball from left to right – one can do so just as effectively by using the outside of the top of the right boot. It is slightly more difficult to execute with accuracy than the shot with the inside of the foot, but these days many top professionals can achieve considerable accuracy and can gain even greater power with this method.

The ball must be struck on the 'inside', i.e. on the left-hand side for the right-footed shot, the right leg sweeping across the face of the ball to make contact. This will cause the ball to spin in its trajectory and serve from left to right.

The more upright the position of the foot on impact, the more power can be generated, so if the ball is slightly off the ground the maximum of force and swerve can achieved. The foot 'brushes' the ball rather than wrapping round it, making this shot easier to execute when on the run than the shot using the inside of the foot. By using one or other of the techniques outlined here, each foot can swerve the ball in both directions.

● Notice how the player's body has moved around by well over 90 degrees from its original position. This has been caused by the follow-through, which is essential to get extra curl on the ball.

● The ball has come back from outside the goal and out of the reach of the diving goalkeeper.

Power shooting

Most goals are scored from inside the penalty area, but a tight defence can make it hard for even the best striker to get in the box. If the 18-yard box is well guarded, the best chance for scoring is a powerful shot from distance. All too often, long range shooting is a case of hit and hope that results in nothing more than embarrassment and lost possession. However with a little composure and a lot of practice, you too can start scoring with 25-yard screamers.

In recent years many players have scored spectacular goals with strikes from distance, but nobody has matched the consistently accurate and powerful strikes of Dutchman Ronald Koeman. The former Barcelona and Holland sweeper developed a faultless technique which brought him goals from both free-kicks and open play.

Striking the ball

Timing, rather than muscle, is the key to powerful shooting. To strike the ball well, you will need to position your body so that you can easily connect with the 'sweet spot' on the top of the striking foot. The non-kicking foot should be planted firmly alongside the ball to give you a solid base to generate the necessary power in your kicking foot. Strike through the ball in a continuous motion and, to keep the shot down, position your head directly over the ball. If you swipe at the ball and lean back with your head in the air – as many players do – the ball will end up ballooning over the bar rather than nestling in the net.

Don't panic

An important element when shooting is to keep your eye on the ball. Do not be overcome by excitement, or your desire to see the net bulge, and lift your head too soon – that is a recipe for an inaccurate shot and subsequent embarrassment. If the toe is kept well down when impact is made with the ball, the top of the boot will make an almost flat surface to contact the ball. A long flat follow-through will provide a longer period of control and ensure that the maximum degree of accuracy is attained.

Top tip

● Don't be afraid to try your luck from long range as you may catch the goalkeeper napping. Once you've decided to shoot, strike the ball with conviction and confidence.

● The non-kicking foot is planted alongside the ball, the head is over the ball and the outstretched arm provides extra balance.

'Shooting on sight'

When to shoot is an important consideration for a player. In top televised football it is not unusual to see a team's top striker shooting with almost every opportunity he gets, even though it appears that a team-mate seems to be in a better position and making the pass a more promising option. The striker is rarely blamed for this, because footballers recognise that passing the ball is often passing the buck, and that in the hurly-burly of a football match it is not a bad habit to shoot for goal whenever you are in a scoring position. You might wait a long time for another chance.

There is another advantage to be gained from 'shooting on sight'. It is a positive action, and even if the shot is wayward or straight at the keeper there is always the chance of a ricochet or deflection, or the keeper pushing the ball out to a team-mate.

Surprise is a useful element in power shooting, so hit the ball first time where possible. Taking the extra touch alerts the opponents to your intentions. For the same reason try not to exaggerate your backlift.

Although it may seem a contradiction in a section headed 'power shooting', do not necessarily strive to blast the ball as hard as you can. A quick, sharp, first-time strike will usually be more effective than a harder shot that is 'telegraphed' to the defence.

● Strike through the ball with conviction, still keeping your head down. Don't just hit and hope; go for accuracy as well as power.

● The sight of a prostrate goalkeeper and a bulging net is a great feeling for any striker.

One-v-one

Rounding the keeper

Faced with an advancing keeper, a striker's options are limited: shoot as he comes off his line, chip him as he goes to ground or try to go around him. All too often players hesitate and are forced into the last option and, because of their hesitancy, they make a mess of it. However, going round the keeper is an excellent option providing you're decisive.

As you approach the keeper you must watch his every move. Try to tempt him to dive and commit himself – one way to do this is to feign to shoot. Alternatively you can give the keeper a good sight of the ball. As he tries to dive towards it you must be ready to get the ball out of his reach. You should also try to get your body in his way. By doing this he will either end up stranded or will be forced to foul you and concede a penalty. With the goal at your mercy you must now strike the ball firmly into the middle of the goal. Avoid showing off or delaying your shot. Showboating can be costly – you may end up being closed down by a defender, or worse still miss the target altogether.

1. The keeper rushes off his line to close down the striker who is bearing down on goal.
2. The striker rolls his foot over the ball as the keeper dives and brings it out of the goalie's reach.
3. The keeper is left stranded and the striker wastes no time in stroking the ball into the unprotected net.

Only the keeper to beat and he must score... but only if he keeps his cool. All too often strikers freeze in one-against-one situations and miss their chance. The art of good finishing is to stay in control and to wait for a good sight of goal before shooting.

The chip technique

Chipping the ball over an onrushing keeper requires the same kind of calm and skill as rounding the keeper. However, with this technique you must send the keeper down earlier as you must make sure you have enough space to get the ball over him and back down beneath the cross bar. The best way to get the keeper to commit himself is to feign to shoot. As the keeper hits the deck you can use either a chip or a scoop (see page 90) to put the ball into the net.

1. Don't be put off as the goalie charges toward you. Delay your shot until he is on his way to ground.
2. Jab at the ball without any follow-through to send it up and over the stranded keeper.
3-4. The goalkeeper had committed himself and is helpless as the ball loops over him and into the unguarded net.

Top tip

● Don't panic and change your mind as the keeper comes out. The chances are that if you try and shoot he'll be in a position to block.
● Try to deceive the keeper into thinking that you are going to strike the ball early by shaping to shoot and stubbing your foot into the ground.

SET PLAYS 6

Nothing gives a coach more satisfaction than the sight of a goal scored from a well-worked set-piece, however, there is also no surer way to irritate 'the boss' than to squander a set-piece opportunity with a hurriedly-taken and ill-considered move.

Short throws

Long throws can put opponents under pressure, but in most circumstances a short and firm throw to a team-mate's feet is the best option. The priority is to retain possession from the throw. The responsibility for keeping possession does not only lie with the taker but also with his team-mates, who must make themselves available to receive the ball.

Players waiting to receive a throw should not stand rooted to the spot, for this makes it easy for their opponents to mark them. They should look for space and make their opponents think about their positions and intentions. Players should keep moving and changing direction. They will lose their markers this way and, providing the thrower has read their intentions, they will be in a good position to receive the ball and retain possession for the team.

The thrower, too, when he has taken the throw, must get in a position to receive the ball. A popular and effective throw-in routine is for the taker to throw the ball and the receiver to lay it back to the thrower's feet. A quick throw-in can also be useful, so a player should retrieve the ball quickly when it goes out of play, assess his options and make a swift decision about the possible advantage of a quick throw.

Taking a throw-in

Many players get penalised for 'foul throws'. So remember the basics:

- Stand with both feet behind the line
- Keep both feet in contact with the ground at all times
- Take the ball right behind your head before releasing. This enables you to throw it rather than push.

1. **Team-mate drops off marker and comes towards the ball.**
2. **Throw is delivered to team-mate who returns the ball to the thrower.**
3. **The thrower now has the ball under control at his feet.**

Throw-ins are an important part of the modern game. In recent years, certain players have developed their throwing to such an extent that a throw-in anywhere in the opponents' half constitutes a goalscoring opportunity. The long throw is employed by many teams and can be as dangerous as a corner kick. Most full-backs will try to develop a long throw as it is such a tremendous asset to their team.

The long throw

The long throw is a potent attacking weapon, but if over-used it becomes predictable and defenders have a better chance of combating its potential threat. The use of the long throw-in is widespread and many clubs employ a long-throw expert.

The long throw is used anywhere from mid-way in the opponents' half up to the corner flag and the thrower's intention is to land the ball somewhere around the penalty spot or six-yard line. A powerful, accurate throw can be very difficult to defend against.

Tips

The success of a long throw depends both on the length and accuracy of the delivery, and the understanding and awareness of team-mates in the goal-mouth.

1. Concentrate on finding a team-mate and not just hurling the ball as far as you can.
2. To improve the distance on your throw develop your technique and practise on a regular basis.
3. Remember, you throw with your back as well as your arms so try to develop a whiplash movement as you deliver the ball.
4. Get as much power behind the ball as you can by using your fingers as well as your hands and arms.
5. Follow through powerfully with your arms.

1. Try to deliver the throw hard and flat rather than looping the ball high.
2. At least one attacker should move to the near post to flick the ball on towards the far post.
3. The remaining attackers must time their runs to attack the ball as it is flicked on towards the far post.

② Free Kicks

Opportunity knocks

It may sound easy to score with an unchallenged shot from the edge of the box, but when there are 11 opponents – plus a few team-mates – between you and the goal the task is not so simple. In most cases, the defending goalkeeper will arrange a wall between himself and the ball, before taking up a sensible position on his line. Faced with a defensive wall 10 yards away which guards one half of the goal, and a goalkeeper positioned to protect the other half, your shot will have to be both accurate and well struck.

The most obvious way of scoring direct from a free-kick is by bending the ball 'around' the defensive wall using the inside of the boot. A ball hit with pace is more likely to beat a goalkeeper. However, the distance from goal, the position of the wall and the agility of the keeper may not allow you to do this. In such cases, a chip, or a floated shot over the wall – aiming for the corner of the goal may be the answer. Either way, free-kicks require an endless amount of practice before use in matches. Even if you are not your team's expert, you should still practise your free-kicks.

It is estimated that around a third of all goals are scored from free-kicks taken around the penalty area. Considering this statistic, it's little wonder that professional clubs practise these dead-ball situations on a regular basis in training. If you're skilful enough, a free-kick near the 18-yard box is a goal-scoring opportunity. Even with a solid and well-positioned wall and an agile goalkeeper these positions can lead to goals... you just need to know what you're doing.

● This popular free-kick routine is difficult to defend against if performed accurately. An attacker (in red) is positioned on the end of the wall and as the kicker approaches the ball, he peels away. The ball is then played over the gap left by the red decoy and into the corner of the net. Like all set pieces this routine must be practised before use in a match.

'Banana kick'

The South Americans are the past masters when it comes to curling free-kicks. As far back as the 1950s Garrincha started the trend with his famous 'banana kick'. The theory is simple, you aim the ball wide of the goal, around the wall, but with enough bend to bring it back on target and into the net. In practice it is not that simple and like all football skills practice is exactly what you'll need if you want to perfect the 'banana kick'.

Basic technique

- Assess the position of the wall and the keeper.
- Pick the spot where you intend to put the ball – and stick to it.
- You should be looking to place the ball just inside one of the posts, in other words as far from the keeper as possible
- In order to do this, aim the ball a couple of feet outside the post and allow the curl you put on the ball to bring it back.
- If you're right-footed, strike the ball with the outside of your foot to bend it from left to right or with the inside of the foot to bend it right to left.
- Strike the left half of the ball to bend it away to the right.
- Graze your foot across the ball and exaggerate the follow-through with your kicking leg.

Developing your kicks

- Concentrate on accuracy first.
- Once you are consistently hitting the target, try to bend the ball.
- The final stage is to increase pace without losing accuracy.

Take your time

The worst free-kicks are those taken quickly by a player seeking to catch defenders out of position. In most cases, his team-mates are not ready either. The first rule of free-kick taking is 'think before you act.' Time is on your side, so go through what was rehearsed on the training ground. Nothing infuriates a coach more than a free-kick, practised and rehearsed over and again in training, but not employed in a match. Remember, it is the defending team which has the problem. Don't solve it for them.

● Don't just hit a hopeful ball forwards or an aimless cross. Take your time and consider your options carefully.

Not all free-kicks (those for obstruction, for example) around the box are direct and some are from such an angle that a shot at goal is not a serious option. But any free-kick in the last third of the field, irrespective of the angle, is potentially dangerous.

Keep it simple

Do not try to over-complicate free-kicks. A complex move involving four players, one stepping over the ball, one touching the ball, another stopping it and finally the last player hitting it may look technically mind-blowing but will, more often than not, be ineffective. The more players involved the greater the chance of the move breaking down, preventing you getting a shot in on goal. You also give your opponents more time to close down. A simple touch to the side, to take the ball away from the wall, and a clinical shot from a team-mate is more likely to bring a positive result than an elaborate routine.

The passing option

If the defending side has put five or six men in the wall they will probably be outnumbered elsewhere in the box. There is a good chance of finding a team-mate in space in the area, so consider taking a short free-kick rather than opting for the more predictable punt forward.

Play to your strengths and don't waste the opportunity. If you have a neat skilful player, try to play him into the penalty area; he may be able to get a shot in, or, he may tempt an opponent into a wild tackle and earn you a penalty. Alternatively, if you have players who pose a threat in the air, put the ball in high. However, don't become too predictable; vary your delivery.

● In this situation everybody expects a high-ball to the far post. However in this case the ball is delivered hard to the near post. The attacker catches the defenders napping and sneaks in to score.

4

Flick-up and volley free-kick

In an English First Division match between Coventry City and Everton in the 1970s, Coventry's Ernie Hunt and Willie Carr caused a soccer sensation with an astonishing free-kick move which had never been seen before.

The pair stood by the ball just outside the penalty area, a wall of yellow-shirted Everton players lined up protecting the goal in front of them. A clever curler around the wall....a powerful drive through it....or perhaps a gentle chip over the top....just what did they have in mind? The answer was something few, if any, had witnessed before. Carr stood over the ball, with a foot either side, facing the touch line while Hunt lined up to take a shot.

On the referee's whistle, ginger-haired Carr squeezed the ball in between his feet and, in one subtle movement, flicked the ball gently into the air inviting Hunt to volley the ball goalwards, which he did with aplomb. Whether the Everton keeper was deceived by the trickery of Carr's move or the power of Hunt's shot is hard to say, but the end result was a spectacular goal that was to be replayed time and time again.

Soon after, an another English First Division match Southampton pair Peter Osgood and Jim McCalliog attempted an alternative version. Osgood, stood just outside the penalty area to the right of the goal and provided the subtlety with a gentle flick, scooping the ball into the air while McCalliog ran in to volley home. The nature of the two 'flick and volley' free kicks caused alarm amongst the English Football Association which deemed that such 'trickery', not skill, was unlawful and not in the spirit of the game.

1-3. **The player on the ball takes a short free-kick to a team-mate standing in front of him. The receiving player flicks the ball up into the air as his colleague prepares to volley the ball goalwards. The speed of the control and the flick is paramount because the defenders in the wall will try to close down the impending shot.**

Breaking the law

The current rule on free-kicks states that:

'The ball shall be in play when it has travelled its own circumference.'

This means that if the ball is flicked up before it has first rolled along the ground, it is not in play and, therefore, cannot be struck by another player. Effectively, the Hunt and Carr style free-kick is now outlawed. However, do not despair, because the variation of this set-play, which is demonstrated here, is both devastating and completely legal.

4-6. **The main benefit of this particular free-kick is that the player volleying the ball can strike it so that it clears the wall and dips goalward. It is also possible to generate more power from a volley and the defenders in the wall are left taking evasive action as the ball flies past.**

5

The passed free-kick

When taking a free-kick just outside the opposition's penalty area, there are a number of options open to an attacking team. We have already talked about the flick-up and volley and the bending free-kick as direct approaches, but there will be times in a game when something other than the straightforward shooting option should be considered. If the distance from goal is too great, the angle is too acute or there are simply too many defenders in the wall or on the line for you to get in a decent strike, then this is where the passed free-kick comes into play.

Dummying the wall

This type of free-kick depends upon convincing the defending team that you are going to shoot for goal. If you can do that, it's a fair bet that you will catch them unaware and ill-equipped to combat the movement of your attacking players.

One of the most effective routines for this type of free-kick works by playing the ball down the side of the wall to team-mate who has made what appears to be a dummy run over the ball. Defenders are invariably left flat-footed by this routine, and usually elect not to bother tracking an opponent who seems to be making the now-standard decoy run over the ball prior to a team-mate having a shot on goal. A side-foot pass down the side of the wall is usually enough to find the 'decoy-runner', who is now in possession of the ball deep inside your opponents' penalty area.

● There are three white-shirted attacking players involved in this move – the passer (centre), the receiver (left) and the striker (right).

● The defence is now completely confused and the striker finds himself in the clear with only the keeper to beat.

● The defenders in the wall believe the taker will go directly for goal, but instead he passes to the receiver who has made an early run into the box.

● The striker, who had positioned himself on the edge of the opposition wall, now spins away from the static defenders and runs to collect the second pass.

● The ball nestles in the net and the red team are left to explain their chaotic defending to their manager.

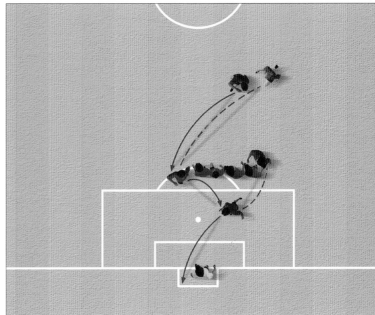

● This birds-eye-view diagram shows how the passed free-kick works. Broken lines represent runs made off the ball, while solid lines are passes and shots.

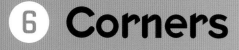

6 Corners

The biggest mistake players make when taking corner kicks is to just hit the ball high into the penalty area and hope it finds a team-mate. That is not good enough and a waste of a good opportunity. Watch a decent player taking a corner and you will see that he has a plan in mind, a particular player he is trying to pick out.

There are many options open to a corner kicker, but the three most commonly used are:
1. the near post corner
2. the quickly taken, short corner
3. the far post corner

No matter which option you take, your priority should be to make the cross as difficult for the keeper to deal with as possible. A floated corner aimed towards the six-yard box, for example, is easy for any keeper to catch. If there is no real pace on the ball it will be simple for the keeper to come and claim the cross. For the attacking side this is a total waste of a good situation.

The near-post corner

The near-post corner is particularly difficult for goalkeepers to deal with. The first ball (the corner itself) cannot be reached by the keeper, who is forced to rely on his team-mates to defend the situation. The ball should be delivered high to the near post and onto the head of an attacker. If the delivery is good, the ball will be flicked on by the attacker (though often a defender will inadvertently flick the ball on in an effort to clear the danger) into a dangerous area where team-mates will be trying to attack the ball and put it in the net. By the time the ball has been flicked on, the defenders are unsure where the ball is heading and the keeper is rooted to his line.

The near-post corner is extremely effective, but the key to good corner-taking is to vary your delivery so that your opponents are kept guessing. The short corner delivers the ball at a different angle and the far-post corner offers numerous options.

● A good near-post corner must be driven in hard and not too high.

● This diagram reveals not only the simplicity but also the effectiveness of the near-post corner. Player A delivers the ball onto the head of player B. At the same time, Player C makes a run forward, meeting the flick and heading into the net.

A

B

C

● The player flicking the ball on must get in front of his marker and time his jump so that the ball lifts off his head toward the far post.

● Forwards attacking the flick must make positive, early runs. They must also concentrate on keeping the ball down if they get a shot or header in on goal.

Corners – short and long

The short corner

The short corner is particularly useful if your team lacks players who are strong in the air. A team-mate makes a run from the near post towards the corner flag, receives a short pass and returns the ball to the corner taker who can deliver his cross (either high or low) from a different angle. By this time, attacking team-mates should have made their move and given the corner kicker the option of going for the near or far post.

The defenders will also have been pulled out of position and a decent cross could result in a goal. The only peril of the short corner is the risk of off-side. Defending teams can be quick to push out, so if you receive the ball from a short corner, don't be tempted to return it to the kicker if he is still ahead of you… flags might be waved and an opportunity lost. A poorly delivered corner is frustrating for everyone, so make sure you take your time and hit a quality ball into the box.

Tips

● Time your delivery so that it coincides with the runs of team-mates
● Strike the ball with pace to make it difficult to defend against
● Carefully consider your options. If the opposition are strong in the air, play a short corner to work the ball into the box

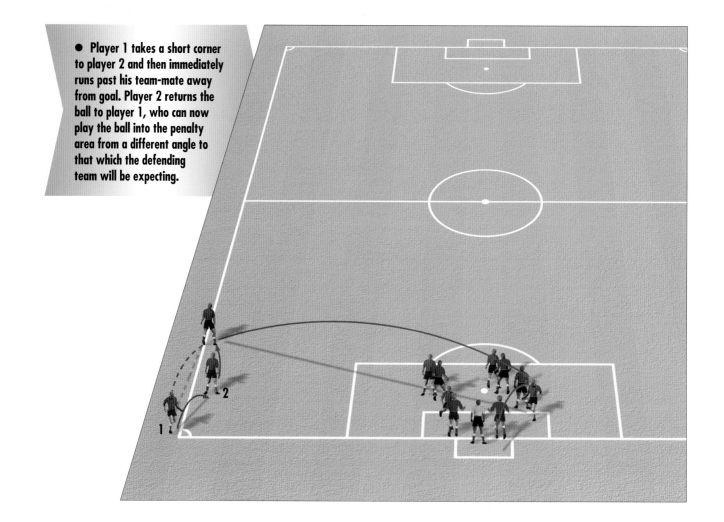

● Player 1 takes a short corner to player 2 and then immediately runs past his team-mate away from goal. Player 2 returns the ball to player 1, who can now play the ball into the penalty area from a different angle to that which the defending team will be expecting.

The far-post corner

The far-post corner is a more straight forward option to the short corner. A basic delivery – struck with pace to leave the keeper guessing as to whether he has time to come for it or not – is aimed for a team-mate at the back post. This is where the best headers of the ball should be positioned. Even if the ball is delivered properly, the attacker at the far post must still get enough power on the ball to beat the keeper. In most cases a left-footed player will take corners from the right (curling the ball in towards goal) and a right-footed player from the left. However, this can make life easy for the keeper, so vary the delivery so that some swing in while some swing out and away from the keeper's reach.

A header from a far-post corner doesn't always produce a goal directly, but a header towards goal can cause chaos and confusion for the defence. But corners are not just about the kicker and 'the big guy in the middle'. Others on the attacking side play their part too. If you are taking a far-post corner, some of the smaller players should make runs towards the near post as decoys. This will distract defenders and make space for team-mates. There is also the chance that some of these decoy players will be on hand to latch onto any knock-downs or spilled shots.

●ost corners must be delivered with enough pace and height to elude the goalkeeper.
●n the ball from a far-post corner attackers must drop off their markers and time their runs to
●t precisely the right time.

Think positively

Decide where you are going to strike the ball before you put it down, and don't change your mind. Indecision is likely to result in a poor penalty. Only step up to strike the ball when you are composed. At this point, you must feel confident that you will strike the ball well enough for it to reach it's intended target – the back of the net.

A player can practise taking penalties all day long, but there is little to prepare him for being thrust into a position where victory or defeat is solely down to him. It can be a frightening prospect. Who would have liked to have been a player in the shoot-out for the 1994 World Cup final in the USA. The pressure must have been immense. Some players thrive on that 'winner takes all' situation, preferring to consider the prospect of scoring and being hailed a hero than missing and being damned as the villain.

Keep it down

Whatever you do, try to keep your head down. There is nothing worse than skying a penalty over the bar. At least if you make the keeper save the ball there is the chance of a rebound. The closer you place the ball into the corners, the more difficult it will be for even the best goalkeeper to save it.

Most players favour the 'placed' penalty, struck low with the side of the foot into your chosen corner of the net. Some players have even added a little shimmy to their run up in an effort to entice the keeper to commit himself before the ball is struck. There is an element of risk in this approach and it requires supreme confidence. Care must also be taken not to break your run up as this is against the rules.

In recent years the 'blasted' penalty has become a popular option among certain strikers. The majority of keepers tend to commit themselves to a desperate, full length dive either way, so a direct route down the middle of the goal, using power, can be effective. If you choose this option, you must keep your head down and over the top of the ball to prevent your shot flying high over the crossbar.

● The side-foot penalty high to the keeper's right- or left-hand side is the most common and, over the years, the most effective. Concentrate on hitting the ball cleanly and positively towards the selected corner, using the side of your strongest foot as shown.

Top Tip

● Do not look at the goalkeeper on your run up as he will do anything he can to put you off.

The best players do not necessarily make the best penalty-takers. It is usually the player who holds his nerve best who is the penalty king. The basic skill of beating a goalkeeper from 12 yards is not difficult, but in the context of a highly competitive football match it can be daunting. And with the introduction of penalty shoot-outs to settle cup matches there are more and more of these nerve-tingling scenarios at all levels of the game.

The Chipped penalty

A penalty is a keeper's best chance to become a hero, so you can be sure that he'll make every effort to pull off a save. In most cases, keepers are so keen that they move early and dive, full-stretch, in one direction or the other. To the coolest of strikers, this gives the opportunity to score with one of the cheekiest moves in the game – the chipped penalty. As the keeper dives, the striker just chips the ball straight into the middle of the goal and over the prostrate keeper. Couldn't be more simple. However, the danger with this technique is that if the goalkeeper stands up in the middle of his goal he can easily catch the ball and make the striker look a fool.

● Try to deceive the keeper by looking at the corner of the goal.

● Watch the keeper's position on your run-up – he should start to move. Look at the ball as you strike it.

● Stab at the ball and don't follow through.

● The keeper dives out of the way and the ball nestles in the net.

Tips

1. When you have decided where to put your penalty, do not change your mind on your run up. The results can be woeful.
2. Look at the goal before you take the kick, but look at the ball when striking. Keep your head down to avoid 'skying' the ball.
3. If you are going for accuracy rather than power, make sure you place the ball as near to the post as possible.
4. Be positive and remain focused.

It's good to talk

If you see an opponent making a run that has gone unnoticed by the player marking him, it's up to you to alert your team-mate to the danger. Keep looking around while waiting for the kick or throw to be taken, and always be ready to speak up in the team cause.

Fundamentals

Defending from set-pieces is not a complicated business. Get the fundamentals right and you should have no trouble. The key is to mark every player – including the kicker – and to stay with your man wherever he goes. It is also important to remember to mark your opponent on the side nearest the goal (goal-side).

Corners

It is always wise to position a player on each post when defending at a corner. As the kick is taken, the player on the near-post should stand facing the corner-taker, although, he will need to turn around to position himself inside the post once the ball arrives in the penalty area. The player at the far post should start from a position inside the post and facing the kicker before turning to face the halfway line once the kick is taken. A defender should also be positioned as close to the kicker as the ref will allow (the rules state this should be 10 yards).

The remaining defenders should vary their positions according to the actions of the attacking team. For example, if a group of attackers assemble at the near post, then so too must a like-number of defenders. However, in all cases, the defending team should make sure that they have a man in front of the first attacker. One of the most difficult tactics to defend against is a player who arrives late in the box. If a defender tries to run with the attacker he is likely to be forced to head the ball toward his own goal, but if he takes up a position early and waits for the ball, he is likely to be out-jumped by the attacker who has the benefit of a run up. In this situation it is best to go for safety first, so run with the attacker and try to get the ball out of play, even at the expense of a corner.

Defending teams will often struggle to combat short corners. This is because all-too frequently nobody bothers to run with a player who goes towards the corner taker. It is assumed that the man marking the kicker can deal with this situation, but that is not so, as he is now marking two players instead of one.

● **A good defensive formation ahead of a corner from the left. The goalkeeper is protected by a man on each post, along with defenders in front of the taker and on the edge of the six-yard box.**

1-2. **The blue defender on the near post holds her position until the last minute, but once she is sure she will win the ball she moves out decisively and heads it clear.**

Most football managers take the view that any goal conceded at a set-play is one given away too cheaply. Such 'soft goals' almost always result in a post-match inquest, at which defenders and goalkeeper are heavily censured. The reason that coaches take such a hard line on defending set-plays is that this aspect of the game requires no great skill, merely organisation and concentration. Put simply, if everybody marks a man and stays with him, the opposition will need to produce something more than a little spectacular to create a goalscoring opportunity.

Free-kicks

For free-kicks in wide areas the same principles as used to defend corners should be applied. However, with free-kicks conceded within shooting range, the defending team faces an altogether different prospect. When the free-kick is given, the first thing you must discover is whether the kick is direct or indirect (the referee will indicate an indirect free-kick by holding his arm aloft). If the kick is indirect you will need to designate a player to close down the shot as soon as the ball is played. However, whether direct or indirect, you must set up a defensive wall. According to the rules, all defenders must be 10 yards from the ball and the referee will indicate this distance to the defending team. The goalkeeper must then position the wall to cover one half of his goal, allowing him to concentrate on the remainder of his goal himself. The number of players needed in the wall will vary according to how close the kick is to goal (as a general rule, the closer to goal the more players will be needed). One player should turn to face the keeper as the wall is being arranged, but once it is set the wall must remain solid.

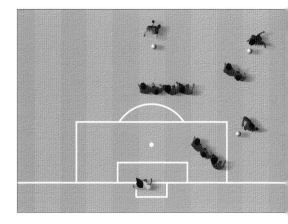

● **The three walls illustrated above, demonstrate how different circumstances call for walls of varied sizes and positions.**

Throw-ins

As with a corner, every opponent, including the taker, should be marked from a throw-in. For long throw-ins, a player should be positioned on either side of the first attacker to prevent him from flicking the ball on at the near post.

● **The blue shirted number 2 delivers a short throw into her team-mate's feet.**

● **The receiver controls the ball, but is under pressure and opts to lay the ball back to the thrower.**

● **Both thrower and receiver are well marked, and as the ball is returned to the thrower, a red-shirted defender nips in and wins possession for her team.**

TACTiCAL PLAY

7

All footballers, whatever their position, need to appreciate what their coach expects of them on the pitch. No matter how fit and how skilful you are, your talents need to be directed and properly utilised.

1

Your role in the team (defenders)

Know your job

Footballers are usually pigeon-holed as defenders, midfielders or attackers, but these three categories do not tell the whole story. Each category is sub-divided and particular teams and particular managers will interpret each position in a different light. For example, in some teams strikers will not be expected to do much by way of tracking back, whereas in other teams the centre-forward will be regarded as the first line of defence and will have to close down opponents and tackle back. Any good coach will make his expectations clear to you, but you can always ask if you're not sure.

Defenders (full-backs)

It's a myth that defenders don't have to be fit. In the past, there may have been some truth in this, but nowadays defenders are expected to join in attacks, support their midfielders and get back to do their own job. Full-backs, and wing-backs in particular, need a great deal of stamina. This role requires you to cover a great deal of ground. In some systems you will be expected to cover the whole flank – operating as a winger when you're attacking and tracking back and covering like an orthodox defender.

Training for full-backs is very similar to midfielders. At professional level, full-backs and wing-backs use specially designed parachutes to build up their stamina and work rate. These parachutes are attached to the players and offer a solid resistance to their legs which makes them stronger and quicker to react. Full-backs wear them for repeated runs of 50 yards. Similar running exercises are carried out while wearing weighted jackets (see page 22) – these jackets make the player carry an extra 10 per cent of his body weight. If you can't get hold of specialist items like weight jackets and parachutes, an ordinary jacket with weight in the pockets, or a car tyre attached to a belt via a rope can work just as well. Power training with weight jackets and parachutes is extremely strenuous and so you must consider the age of the players you are working with. Do not ask a 32-year-old to produce the same results as a 16-year-old. Older players must be allowed greater time for recovery than their younger team-mates.

Tailor your training

Although precise roles given to players will vary from team to team, there are still great similarities in the demands and preparation needed for any given position on the field. To this end, training sessions should incorporate some time for smaller groups of players to follow exercises tailored for their role within the team.

1-2. **The bleep test is one way that coaches can assess fitness. The players start running between cones and are paced by a bleep sound. The bleeps get progressively faster until each player is forced to stop.**

To make the most of your ability, you must gain an awareness of your role within the team. It is down to the team coach to clarify what exactly is expected of you on match days, but it is down to you to make sure that you are properly prepared and able to fulfil your side of the bargain for those all-important 90 minutes.

Defenders (centre-backs)

In recent years the role of the central defender has become more demanding, as changes to the back-pass rule have required players to work around 10 per cent harder than they did under the old regulations. Pace has also become more important – as strikers get quicker, defenders must speed up to keep up. To develop the pace of central defenders, the same sort of speed endurance work as used for full-backs is recommended. This helps improve their speed over short distances, which is particularly valuable to central defenders who are often faced with situations where they have to turn and run back towards their own goal to track a lively striker.

The weighted jacket is also useful to help develop a central defender's spring. If a player can become accustomed to jumping with a heavy weighted jacket in training sessions, he will find aerial challenges easy on a match day. This training will also improve players' overall fitness and enable them to last longer during a game. Body strength is also important to central defenders. It is essential for them to have enough power to hold players off, particularly the big, bustling centre-forwards who are going to present a physical and aerobic test. Gym work is therefore important for central defenders.

● Heading the ball requires both good upper body strength and a powerful spring. Central defenders, and other players who frequently head the ball, must tailor their training accordingly.

2

Your role in the team (midfielders and attackers)

Midfielders

Midfield players need to develop a high level of stamina. They will be expected to make runs, cover and tackle back for the whole of the game. The only way to prepare for this kind of exertion is to do plenty of running in training. Defensive midfielders, who are going to be involved in aerial challenges and tackles more than attacking runs, should take elements of their training from that recommended for defenders. Similarly, attacking midfielders should concentrate on stamina plus elements from the forwards' programme. Plyometric training (see page 22) is particularly valuable for all midfielders as in the middle of the field you will have to react quickly as the ball is played through congested areas and as attack changes to defence.

1-2. **Some of the best fitness exercises for midfielders incorporate the ball, and in this way they help to improve technique as well as stamina. This exercise requires each player to dribble the ball to a 20-metre mark, turn and run back with the ball, before releasing a 10-metre pass to a team-mate who receives the ball and sets out on the same run. The exercise is repeated after a recovery period while the team-mate completes his run.**

Forwards

Forwards have to be fitter nowadays because they must close down defenders rather than simply hold a central position. Strikers who play up front on their own have to be supremely fit, as they must cover a huge amount of ground. To develop this kind of stamina you'll need to follow a programme of running. Whatever system your team plays, you will need to have good explosive power and acceleration to play up front. Resistance training is the best way to develop this type of speed. Strength, too, is essential for a front man.

● Technique is all important for forwards. Goalscoring opportunities are usually infrequent, so strikers must hone their balance and control in order to maximise any chances that come their way. If the ball arrives at waist-height there will be no time to trap it before shooting, hence it becomes essential to practise skills such as volleying.

As anybody who has watched young children play football will testify, inexperienced footballers are instinctively drawn toward the ball. However, as a tactical ploy, having all 10 outfield players swarming around the ball is neither effective nor entertaining. Fortunately, with the aid of some basic coaching, most teams soon learn to hold a more balanced shape, keeping each player in a designated area of the field.

All too often, though, youthful exuberance and energy is replaced by a static and predictable approach. Instead of using their judgement about whether to make a run forward, players in this mindset will rigidly adhere to the instructions they have been given by their coach. The solution lies in developing a balanced style of play which combines both movement and discipline.

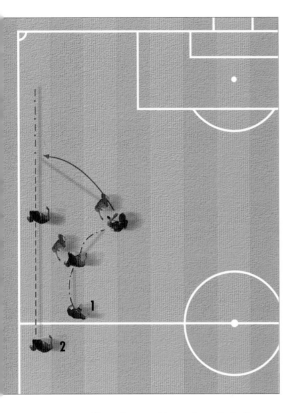

● **Player 1 starts his run from the halfway line and moves forward. His path is blocked by a defender who forces him inside and toward the middle of the pitch. As this is all going on, and undetected by the blue team, player 2 has made his way into the space that has opened up down the left wing. Player 1 spots his team-mate's overlapping run and releases the ball into space for player two to run onto.**

The right movement

Many midfielders and defenders make the mistake of increasing their workrate when defending, and resting when their team is in possession. However, the most valuable players work equally hard whether defending or attacking. If you don't work hard when in possession of the football you will soon lose it.

One sure way to lose possession is to stand waiting for a pass to arrive at your feet. When a team-mate has the ball you should, whenever possible, get in a position to receive the ball. To use coaching jargon, you must 'give him options'. If the player with the ball has nobody to pass to he will be forced to run with the ball or hit a hopeful punt forward into space, and if he has just one 'option' for a pass, it will be easy for the defending team to cut the ball out. To avoid such situations you must make positive runs off the ball into space and away from markers. However, it is no use running too far from your team-mate. Stay within easy passing range and make your position known to the man with the ball. Always tell him exactly where you are. It's no use shouting 'over here John, flick it,' if John can't see where 'over here' is. The following words are commonly used to help explain your location to a team-mate who has his back to you:

1. 'Square – shout this when you're in a line (which runs parallel to the halfway-line) with your team-mate. A square pass is one which goes sideways rather than forward or backward.
2. 'Inside' – use when you're heading for goal in a position between your team-mate and the middle of the pitch. This call is usually used to tell your colleague that you're running forward through the middle of the pitch.
3. 'Outside' – use this shout when you're heading toward your opponent's goal in a position between your team-mate and the nearest touchline. This call is usually used to tell your colleague that you're running down the wing.
4. 'One more' – this shout is used as the ball travels between two team-mates, and tells the player who is about to receive the ball to merely help the pass on in the same direction. All your colleague needs to do is add weight rather than direction to the pass he receives.
5. 'Back door' – use this shout when you're in a position directly behind your team-mate. Usually used to let him know that you want him to backheel the ball to you.

The overlap

One of the most successful and frequently used running-off-the-ball tactics is the overlap. This is where one player (typically a winger) runs with the ball down the wing toward his opponents' goal. The player will usually find his path blocked by a defender as he heads forward, but his team-mate (typically a full-back), having predicted this scenario, is already running. The second player runs down the outside of his team-mate who has the ball and as he gets ahead of him, the player releases a pass down the wing in front of his overlapping colleague. The defender is left flat-footed and has several yards to catch up as he turns to chase the overlapper.

Finding space

The key to good off the ball running is to find space. Try to move into areas where defenders least expect you to go. It is often worth taking the ball away from goal so that when you return the play towards the penalty area, your opponents are moving in the wrong direction. The great thing about running off the ball is that, even if your team-mates opt not to pass to you, your run will almost certainly act as a decoy, drawing defenders away from the ball.

1. **The player with the ball has her path forward blocked by the defender.**
2. **As the player in possession slows, her team-mate comes alongside, running down the wing.**
3. **A simple pass is released into the path of the overlapping attacker.**

Covering for team-mates

The days when only defenders defended, and only forwards attacked are long gone. Today, all players have to be flexible and whether you're a right-back or a centre-forward you will be expected to help out in other areas of the field. Covering for team-mates has become a key feature of the modern game and when a defender or midfielder moves forward, one of his colleagues must plug the gap he or she has left behind.

Responsibilities for covering will, of course, vary according to individual tactics and match situations, but there are a number of standard practices which are commonly employed throughout football.

Diagrams one and two are based on a 4-4-2 system, while diagram three presumes a 3-4-1-2 formation.

1. **Basic cover.** On most occasions, cover should be provided by the player nearest to the 'gap' that needs plugging. This requires awareness of your team-mates' movement and a commitment to the less-glamorous defending side of the game for those who play in the midfield. Diagram 1 shows how the covering should work in a standard 4-2-4 formation. Wingers cover for full backs and advancing centre-backs are looked after by the central midfielders.

1

2. **The right full-back has moved forward to join the attack** and on this occasion the right winger is also involved in the offensive play. If possession is lost and an attack is made down the right, the defence will need to reorganise as a back three unit. The left-back will cover the far post, the left-sided centre-back will move to a more central position and the right-sided centre-back will cover the right flank.

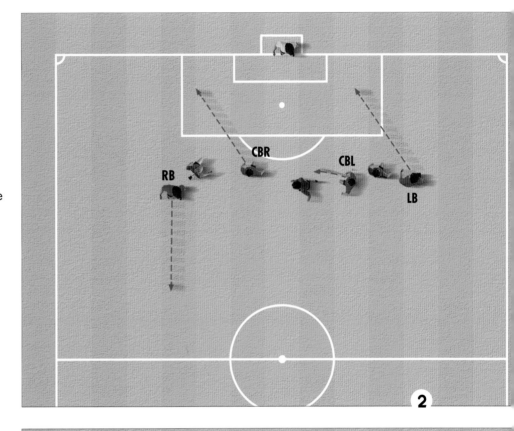

3. **The sweeper system** relies greatly on a pre-determined system of cover. In the example illustrated, the right wing-back has broken forward, but with no winger to cover for him, the job is left to the right-sided centre-back who moves across to the right flank. The changes do not end there though. The sweeper takes up the right-sided centre-back's position while the other centre-back shuffles over too and the left wing-back drops into defence. The net effect is that the defensive unit now takes on a more orthodox four-man appearance.

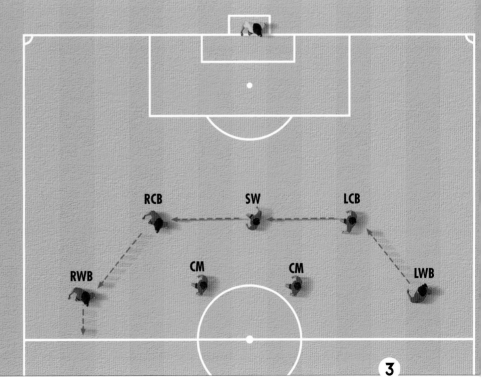

Football Philosophies

A choice of two

There are many different football philosophies but two, in particular, have dominated the modern game:

1. The direct approach

English football has traditionally been associated with the direct approach or, as it is often known, 'Route one'. This football philosophy is based on the assumption that the more times you put the ball in the attacking third of the field, the more goals you will score. As a result, the emphasis of the direct approach is on getting the ball forward quickly into 'danger zones', rather than on passing the ball patiently through midfield.

   Teams that opt for this philosophy are likely to favour strong, fast players who are good in the air, as opposed to smaller more skilful footballers. Most direct teams will look to launch the ball forward toward a big striker (known as a 'target man') at the earliest opportunity. The target man's job is to flick the ball on towards goal and generally create mayhem in the opposition penalty area. Once the target man has challenged for the ball, and whether he has won it or not, the rest of the forward line are expected to challenge for the loose ball (often called the second ball). By putting such physical pressure on your opponent's defence, it is argued, you are likely to force an error and thereby create a goalscoring opportunity.

● It is essential that players pass and move for the possession approach to be successful. A simple passing exchange (as shown here) is one of the most effective ways to move forward while retaining controlled possession. Here player 1 passes the ball into the feet of player 2, but instead of admiring the accuracy of his pass, player 1 immediately runs forward to give his team-mate a simple outlet. Player 2 returns the ball and, as he moves forward, player 1 pushes the ball forward into his path.

Your coach's philosophy on how the game should be played will decide everything from the individual roles of particular players to the team's formation and the type of training you do.

2. Possession football

As the name implies, possession football is based around the value of keeping hold of the ball. It is a style of play that is widely associated with European football, particularly Italian football. Possession football is often described as negative or defensive. This is because it places great stock by the fact that the other team cannot score while you have the ball.

Coaches who favour the possession approach will usually build their team around a skilful midfield playmaker. The playmaker is the key figure in the team. He will dictate the pace of the game, linking defence and attack and instigating passing movements. Whenever possible the ball will be played forward. When a forward pass is not available, a sideways or backward pass will be employed in preference to a hopeful punt forward. This aspect of the possession football style will often irritate supporters, who are usually eager to see the ball played forward, but it is a central premise of the philosophy. The belief is that, although one route to goal is blocked, it is better to build again patiently and work an opening, than to surrender the ball cheaply to the opposition.

Possession football can be frustrating to watch. If both teams opt for this approach the game can rapidly become a cat-and-mouse affair, dominated by posturing rather than any real action as both teams probe for an opening. However, despite this criticism, possession football is widely used at the top level of the game and is also commonly believed to be superior to the more direct approach.

A sporting compromise

Many coaches opt for a pragmatic approach whereby elements of both philosophies are combined. In most cases the result is an approach which is largely based around possession football, but which also gives defenders the freedom to launch the ball forward when the need arises.

● A tight passing circle, with two players trying to intercept, is an enjoyable way to hone your passing skills. This exercise will let you develop your ability to find a team-mate even under extreme pressure.

SYSTEMS OF PLAY

8

Players, rather than tactics, win matches. However, for players to fulfil their potential and play to the best of their abilities, they must have an appreciation of tactics and be able to play within different systems. The whole should be greater than the sum of its parts and the individual efforts of each player must complement the efforts of his team-mates.

① Tactical developments

Evolution of the game

The game of football is constantly evolving. Rule changes and greater fitness have made the game faster at all levels. As a result, tactics have had to evolve at a similarly furious pace.

The back-pass rule, in particular, has affected tactics. Many teams now defend deeper and are unwilling to squeeze up to the half-way line as they used to. More teams play with a sweeper and this also presents coaches and managers with a problem because deep-lying defences are hard to break down. Putting the ball behind defenders and chasing is no longer good enough. In many teams, midfield players have overcome this problem by developing the craft and guile to break down astute defences.

More and more teams are moving away from the traditional 4-4-2 formation and, instead, are using three central defenders – one invariably dropping back – and two wing-backs. Wing-backs are, essentially, full-backs who have been given a licence to push on when their team is in possession. This is the single biggest tactical change football has seen in recent times. A similar change in attacking tactics has seen a return to vogue for the deep-lying striker, who plays just behind an orthodox centre-forward. This position was first made famous more than 40 years ago by the skilful Hungarian Nandor Hidegkuti, a player who was the architect of England's humiliating 6-3 defeat at Wembley in 1953.

The early systems

In the early days of football in the 19th-century, tactics focused almost exclusively on attack. Defences would often consist of a goalkeeper and a full-back, with the remainder of the team comprising an eight-man forward line. A rugby-style offside law, under which all passes played forward were deemed offside, made dribbling the best route to goal. It was, therefore not until the 1880s and the establishment of the three-man offside rule (three men had to be between an attacker and the goal for him to be onside) that rigid tactical systems began to develop.

2-3-5

One of the most successful early systems was known as '2-3-5'. Under this formation, the previously solitary full-back was joined by a defensive partner to form a two-man rearguard. In front of the defence was a three-man half-back line, which comprised a right-half, centre-half and left-half. The half-back line was essentially the midfield, and the centre-half was the team's most important player. He was usually a skilful footballer, with a high level of athleticism and a good passing range. The forward line in the 2-3-5 system was made up of a centre forward, flanked by two inside forwards and two wingers. This formation was extremely popular in Britain, where it dominated the game for the first quarter of the 20th century.

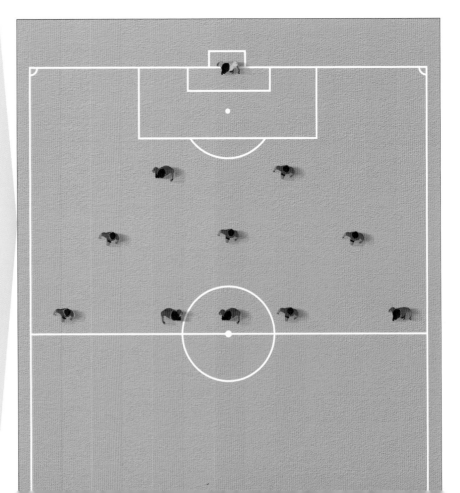

The variety of tactical systems available to coaches today is vast. Every league in every country seems to have a preference for a particular formation. When two systems clash, which regularly happens in European club football and international tournaments, coaches everywhere watch with interest to see which system fares best. In most cases, the quality of the players affects the result much more than the particular system being played, but it is still useful to discover the relative strengths of the different formations.

The W-M formation

In 1925 the offside law was amended so that there only needed to be two – rather than three – opponents between an attacker and goal. Initially, defences struggled to come to terms with this change in the rules. However, in England Arsenal manager Herbert Chapman solved the problem by withdrawing his centre-half, Herbie Roberts, into defence. The new 'third-back' system required the previously attacking centre-half to become a full-time defender, usually taking responsibility for marking the centre-forward. To balance the team, the full-backs were moved out wide to police the opposition wingers, while the inside-forwards were withdrawn into midfield to fill the void left by the centre-half. The W-M formation would remain the orthodoxy in Britain until the late 1950s.

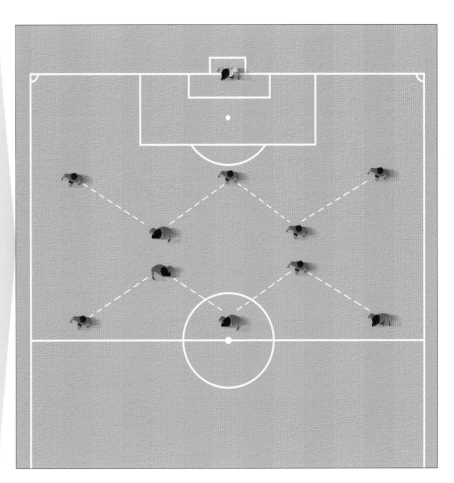

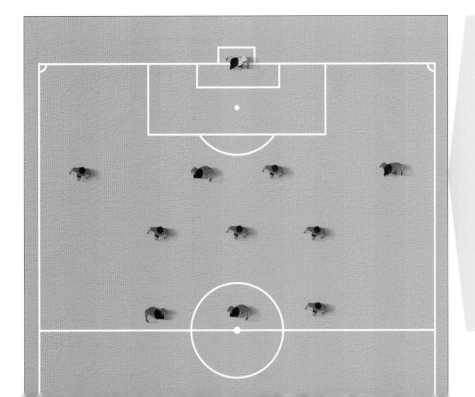

4-3-3

The 4-3-3 system was the formation that took Alf Ramsey's England to victory in the 1966 World Cup final. Under this system, which is still occasionally used today, the full-backs are expected to provide both attacking width and defensive cover. A two man central defence is also employed, thus providing cover for the marauding full-backs. In midfield and attack the 4-3-3 formation is made up of two banks of three, however, the exact responsibilities of these players varies tremendously according to the ideas of individual coaches.

The defensive unit

The foundation of a good 4-4-2 formation is defence. The back four (sometimes described as a flat back four) is made up of two centre-backs and two full-backs. The centre-backs are traditionally strong in the air as they must guard the penalty box from any threatening high balls. The centre-back pairing must develop a good understanding as they do not have the security of a sweeper operating behind them.

The two central defenders are flanked by two full-backs (a left-back and a right-back). The full-backs play an important attacking role, but should not both go forward at the same time. This would leave the two centre-backs exposed to a counter attack. If one of the full-backs pushes on into a forward position, the opposite full-back should tuck in to support the central defensive pairing and, effectively, give the team three men at the back. The raiding full-back supports a midfield that already boasts four players, so the traditional 4-4-2 has now become a more modern 3-5-2. From this example you can see how different tactics can overlap depending on circumstances.

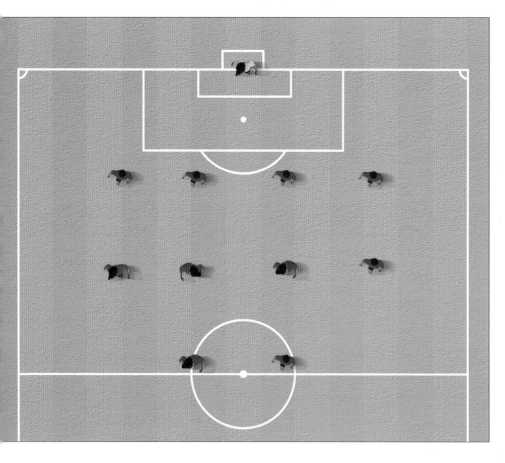

The midfield

The make-up of the midfield in 4-4-2 can be extremely varied. In the past, convention dictated that it should comprise, two wide-men (to patrol the flanks), a ball-winner (to tackle and close down) and a playmaker (to orchestrate attacking moves). Today, things are not so rigid. Some teams play with two ball players and two attacking wingers, while other teams employ two competitive ball-winners and two defensive wide midfielders. Subtle changes in the midfield can turn an attacking formation into a defensive one.

● This formation fits the rectangular shape of the football pitch and allows two 'banks' of four players to get behind the ball and make attacking difficult for opponents.

If there is such a thing as a 'standard system', it's 4-4-2. It uses only two forwards and can, therefore, be a conservative formation. This system is very popular in British football where, until recently, it was universally employed at club level. Coaches and managers like the security offered by four midfielders and four defenders, but 4-4-2 does not have to be a negative system.

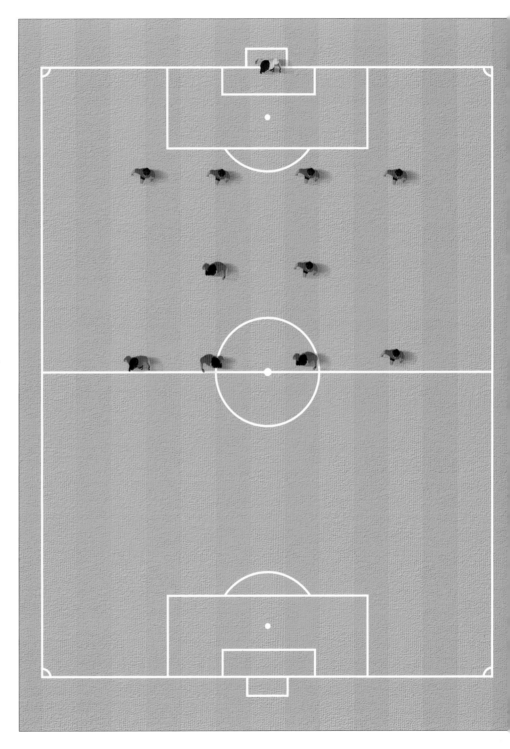

4-4-2 into 4-2-4

A standard 4-4-2 system can quickly be converted to a more attacking 4-2-4 formation by simply pushing the two wide midfielders into more advanced positions, so that they operate as orthodox wingers. The 4-2-4 system is popular in its own right, but it does make great demands of the wide players. To be effective, it depends upon the wingers to get into attacking positions and deliver balls into the box for the strikers to feed upon. The option of playing the ball through the middle of the pitch becomes increasingly difficult, as the two central midfielders are likely to be outnumbered by their opponents.

● The more defensive 4-4-2 system can easily be transformed into a penetrating 4-2-4 system with wide midfielders pushing up level with the two strikers.

Forwards

The role of the two strikers in either 4-4-2 or 4-2-4 is very intensive. The pair must work together, both when in possession of the ball and when defending. The best strikers develop an understanding, so that, for instance, one makes a run to the near post and one to the far post, or one makes a decoy run while the other holds back for a square pass. Both strikers must work particularly hard when the ball is lost. With at least three defenders to pressurise, the importance of closing down effectively becomes paramount. There is no point in strikers charging around and diving at the feet of defenders; all it does is waste energy. Instead, they should close down (see page 48) and force an error. The days of the striker standing with his hands on hips waiting for a pass are long gone.

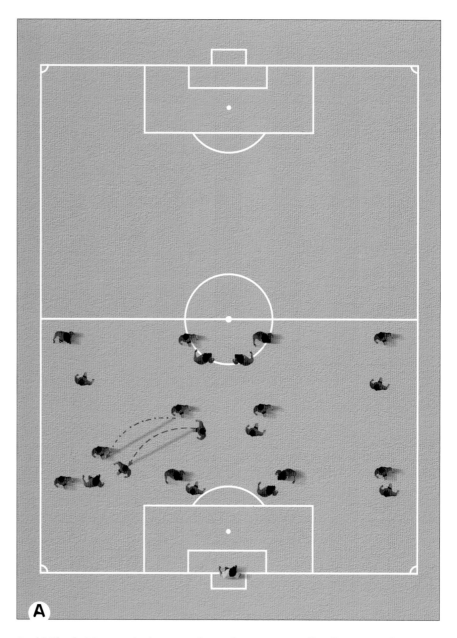

A

A and B. **The decision as whether to mark man-for-man or zonally affects not only a team's defence but also its midfield and attack. Whichever practice you adopt must be followed throughout the team otherwise confusion will reign. The man-marking system is the simpler of the two (as is demonstrated by artwork A). When the red midfielder makes his run forward his blue marker simply tracks him, shepherding him away from goal. However, under the zonal system (artwork B), the red midfielder is tracked part of the way by his blue midfield opponent, before being handed over to the blue team's**

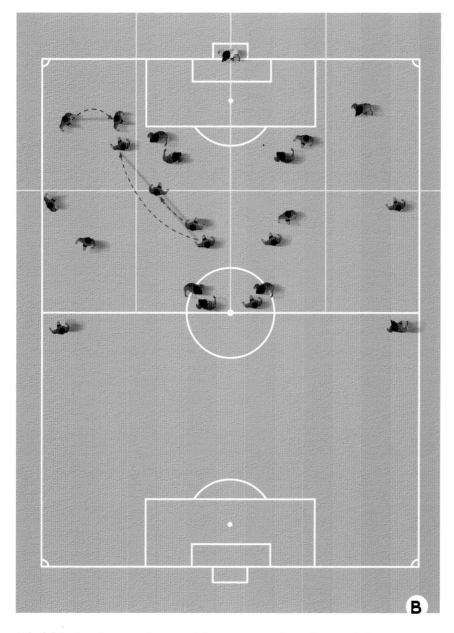

A defensive dilemma

In any formation where you play without a sweeper, the first decision to make is whether to mark zonally or man-for-man. Under the zonal marking system, each defender confines himself to protecting a particular area, whereas man-for-man marking sees each player take an opponent and follow him for the whole game. A real threat to both marking practices, is the striker who drops back into the midfield to pick up the ball. The marker must decide whether to follow him (and thereby leave his central defensive partner alone at the back) or to pass responsibility for marking over to the midfield (though this may leave the midfield outnumbered). The only solution in this situation is to ensure that all opponents are marked and that the team keeps talking on the pitch, so that all players are aware of their changing roles. If just one player fails to appreciate the change you are in trouble.

right full-back as he moves between defensive zones. The problem with this system is that it requires a high degree of communication between team-mates, since if a player has two opponents in his zone he will need to find a willing colleague to help share his workload. In most cases where a team uses the zonal system, a flexible approach is adopted whereby each player starts defending from their designated zones, but once they are tracking a player they stay with that man, irrespective of which zones he runs through.

Sweeper systems

3-5-2 or 5-3-2

This 3-5-2 system has been popular in most of Europe for more than 20 years, but when it was introduced into English football in the 1990s, there were murmurs of discontent and the suggestion was frequently made that the game would become too defensive. The general view was that the emphasis would be on preventing the opposition from scoring, rather than trying to score goals. However, this is not the case and like all systems 5-3-2 is as attacking as the players and coach want it to be. In many cases, teams are happy to attack from a solid base, and with the use of wing-backs (full-backs with licence to get forward) a 5-3-2 formation quickly evolves into an exciting 3-5-2 attacking option.

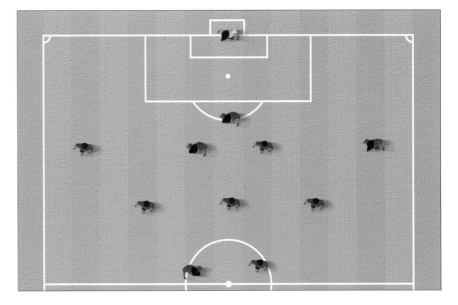

● **The roots of the modern day sweeper system can be found in the Italian Catenaccio system. This formation was based around a four-man defence – marking man-for-man – that also had the added security of a sweeper operating behind the twin centre-backs. Catenaccio was the standard system in Italy throughout most of the 20th century.**

Wing-backs

The role of the wing-back is all important to this formation. To play in this position, you must be extremely athletic (as fit as a traditional central midfielder) and you must have a full understanding of your responsibilities. You will be involved in all aspects of the game and must be proficient at attacking and defending. You must support the midfield and front men when the team is in possession, but quickly revert to defensive duties when possession has been lost. It is a tough job and a demanding position in which to play. But when carried out correctly and successfully, wing-back can be one of the most rewarding positions on the field.

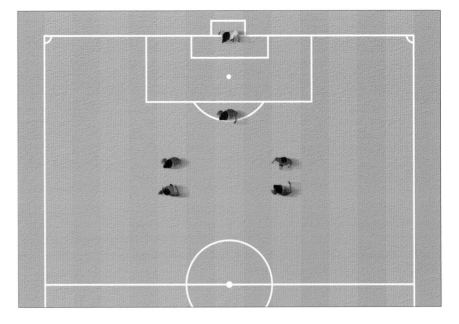

● **The 3-5-2 system has become very popular in England over the last few seasons. It relies upon three central defenders, two of whom mark man-for-man while the other operates in a free role as a sweeper. The sweeper's job, however, is not only a defensive one and he will also be required to step into midfield when the need arises.**

The current vogue in football tactics is for formations based around the 5-3-2 system. This approach gives coaches a degree of security with five defenders, but quickly adapts to an attacking 3-5-2 formation if needed.

5-3-2 v 5-3-2

A game with two teams playing 5-3-2 can be negative. A stalemate can emerge as both teams fail to find gaps in crowded defences. This problem can occur when two teams play the same formation, whatever it is. What should happen, however, is that the team with the better players on the day wins the game. The team that wins the most one-on-one situations all over the park will come out on top in the end. Remember, tactics are only as good as the players who are attempting to carry them out.

The diamond

Coaches and managers have tried variations on a familiar theme from time to time, and the diamond (4-1-2-1-2) system is one such alternative. Essentially, it involves a flat back four with one player sitting just in front of the defence; two central midfield players; a 'floating' attacking midfield player (or a striker operating in 'the hole') and two strikers. This system places a great deal of responsibility on the central midfield players to tuck-in and support the full-backs when they attack down the flanks.

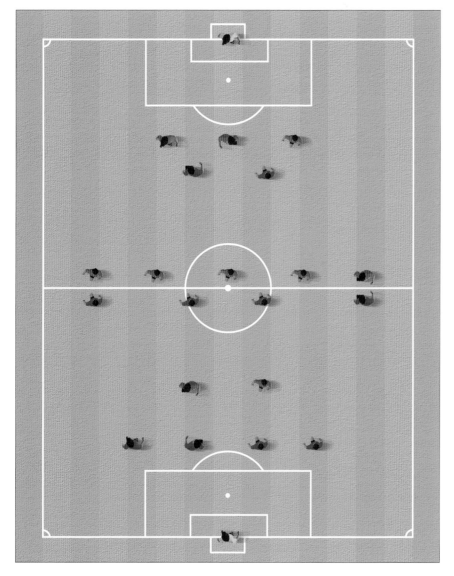

● By adopting this defensive shape (3-5-2), the red team can pack the midfield where they have five men against the blue team's four (who are playing a conventional 4-4-2 system) but still retain two out-and-out strikers.

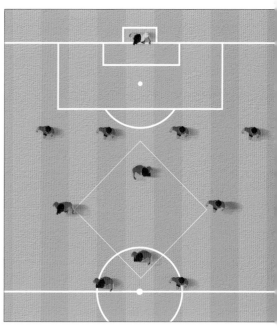

● The diamond is a good system for a passing side, because both full-backs have space in which to attack. However, there are significant disadvantages against the more traditional 4-4-2 or 3-5-2 formations. The main problem is that, unless the two strikers get wide when their opponents have possession, the opposing full-backs will have time and space to build an attack.

LAWS OF THE GAME

9

Football is not a complicated sport. For the most part, the rules of the game are straightforward, and players can usually rely on common sense and a little knowledge to get through a game. However, if you want to make sure that the man in black can't catch you out, it is worth taking the trouble to become familiar with some of football's more complicated rules.

1 Offside

A simple rule

The aim of the offside rule is simple: in short, it is intended to stop forwards from 'goal-hanging'. Without the rule, strikers would just stand in their opponents' penalty area waiting for long balls to be played forward and the game would descend into farce. To avoid this situation, the offside rule requires that to be onside an attacker needs to be nearer to his opponents' goal-line than at least two defenders (one of whom is usually a goalkeeper), at the time when the ball is played forward by a team-mate.

There are several key elements to the offside rule, each of which is worth emphasising, as are a number of notable exceptions:

1. Just because you're in an 'offside position' (e.g. in advance of the last defender with only the keeper between you and goal) you are not necessarily offside. To be 'offside' you must be involved in active play. This means that if you are running back towards your own goal, and away from the action, you are not in breach of the rule.

2. The ball must be played forward for you to be offside, so, if you shoot into an open goal, having received a square pass from a team-mate, the goal will stand.

3. The critical moment is when the ball is actually played forward. It doesn't matter if you are in an offside position when you receive the ball, it's where you were when the ball was played that is important.

4. You cannot be offside from a goal-kick, corner or throw-in.

5. You cannot be offside if you were in your own half when the ball was played forward.

6. You cannot be offside if an opponent plays the ball to you.

Top tip

The offside rule previously stated that a player was offside unless two opponents were between him and the opponents' goal-line. However, the rule has recently been changed in favour of the attacking team, so now a defender level with you could be playing you onside.

Many football fans regard the offside rule as the game's unfathomable conundrum. But in truth, once you strip away the jargon, there's no great mystery behind offside.

● Onside! **The red team are on the attack. Player A attempts to play a square pass to Player B. However, the pass is cut out by the blue defender who deflects the ball forward into the path of player C. Although player C is in an offside position he is deemed to be onside because the ball has not been played forward to him by a team-mate.**

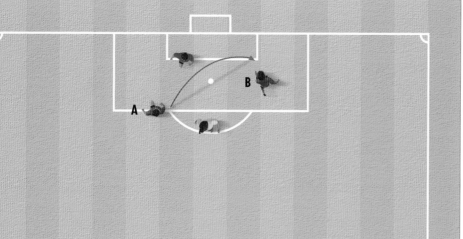

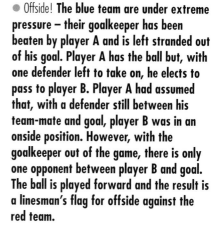

● Offside! **The blue team are under extreme pressure – their goalkeeper has been beaten by player A and is left stranded out of his goal. Player A has the ball but, with one defender left to take on, he elects to pass to player B. Player A had assumed that, with a defender still between his team-mate and goal, player B was in an onside position. However, with the goalkeeper out of the game, there is only one opponent between player B and goal. The ball is played forward and the result is a linesman's flag for offside against the red team.**

● Onside! **Player A has got down the left wing and, in anticipation, player B gets ahead of the blue team defence in the penalty area. Player A crosses the ball to his team-mate who appears to be in an offside position, however, because the ball has not travelled forward, player B is deemed to be onside.**

Direct free-kicks

Direct free-kicks, as the name suggests, are kicks from which the taker may score without the ball having to touch anybody else first. Direct free-kicks must be taken from the place where the incident occurred, except in the event of offences committed by a defending team in their own penalty area, in which case a penalty is awarded rather than a free-kick. There are currently nine offences that bring about the award of a direct free-kick:

1. A kick, or attempted kick, on an opponent
2. Tripping an opponent
3. Jumping at an opponent
4. Charging an opponent in a manner considered by the referee to be either violent or dangerous
5. Charging or tackling an opponent from behind
6. Striking, attempting to strike or spitting at an opponent
7. Holding an opponent
8. Pushing an opponent
9. Handling the ball (this, of course, does not apply to the goalkeeper within his own penalty area)

Red and yellow cards

Many of the nine offences that lead to a direct free-kick can also lead to a booking or a sending-off. However, the use of such sanctions will depend on the directives from individual football associations and the discretion of the referee.

● Handball (far left) and holding an opponent (left) are both fouls that will lead to the award of a direct free-kick.

The free-kick is the most widely used sanction in football, so it is worth getting to know the rules that apply to its use. Free-kicks come in two varieties - direct and indirect - and it is essential for all players to properly understand the distinction.

indirect free-kicks

A goal can only be scored from an indirect free-kick if the ball is touched by more than one player (from either side) on its route to goal. This means that the taker cannot shoot for goal 'direct' from the kick. The referee will indicate the award of an indirect kick by raising his arm above his head. He will keep his arm in this position until the ball is touched by a second player. There are currently 11 offences that lead to an indirect free-kick:

1. Any play that the referee considers to be dangerous (e.g. attempting to kick the ball out of the keeper's hands)
2. Charging fairly (i.e. using the shoulder) but when the ball is not within playing distance
3. Intentionally obstructing an opponent when not playing the ball
4. Charging the goalkeeper
5. When the goalkeeper takes more than four steps while holding the ball
6. When a goalkeeper picks up a ball that was deliberately passed back to him by a team-mate, except where the pass was headed or chested back
7. Time-wasting, including goalkeepers who hold onto the ball for more than five seconds
8. A player caught in an offside position when the ball was played forward
9. Dissent toward the referee
10. Ungentlemanly conduct
11. When a player taking a corner, throw-in or free-kick touches the ball for a second time before any other player touches it

Did you know?

If a player puts the ball directly into his own goal from an indirect free-kick, the referee will award a corner rather than a goal.

● Holding a shirt is usually interpreted as obstruction and results in an indirect free-kick.

Useful rules on free-kicks

1. All opponents must be 10 yards (9.1m) from the ball when a kick is taken.
2. The ball is considered 'in play' when it has travelled the distance of its own circumference. Once in play, the ball can be touched by a second player. In the case of kicks taken by a defending team from inside its own penalty area, the ball must leave the area before it is considered in play.
3. The ball must be stationary when the kick is taken.
4. Free-kicks awarded to a defending team within its own penalty area, can be taken from any other point in the penalty area.

Kick-off

According to the Laws of the game, a match is started by 'a player taking a place kick... into his opponents' half of the field of play'. This event, which is usually referred to as 'kick-off', also takes place after half-time and after a goal is scored. All players must be in their respective halves of the field - with the defending team remaining 10 yards (9.15m) from the centre-spot - until the ball is played forward.

Drop ball

After a temporary break in play, for example when a player is injured as a result of an accident rather than any foul play, the referee will restart the game with what is known as a drop ball. One player from each team is chosen to contest the ball, which is dropped at the place where it was when play was suspended. Neither player is allowed to touch the ball until it has hit the ground, at which point it is deemed in play.

Goal-kick

A goal-kick is given when the whole of the ball, having last been touched by a member of the attacking team, crosses the goal-line (excluding the area between the goal posts). Goal-kicks are taken from any point on the six-yard box and must be kicked into play beyond the 18-yard box. All opposition players must leave the penalty area until the ball has itself left the area. Any player can take a goal-kick, not only the goalkeeper.

● Taking a throw-in should be very straightforward, but its remarkable how many people get penalised for foul-throws. Remember to keep your feet on the ground and behind the line, and always take the ball right back behind your head.

While the ball is in play, football is an uncomplicated sport. However, as soon as the ball leaves the playing area or the game is forced to stop, things become a little less straightforward. There are a variety of ways in which a game can be restarted following a break in play. The method employed by the referee at any particular time will depend on the reason that play was broken.

Throw-in

When the whole of the ball crosses the touch-line, a throw-in is awarded to the team opposed to the player who last touched the ball. The thrower must have both feet on the ground and be standing on the touch-line, or on the ground outside the touch-line, as he delivers the ball. He must hold the ball in both hands and deliver it from behind and over his head. If the throw-in is deemed to be an illegal, or foul, throw, the opposing team will be awarded a throw-in from the same position.

Corner kick

A corner is awarded when the whole of the ball, having last been touched by a member of the defending team, crosses the goal-line (excluding the area between the goal posts). When taking a corner, the whole of the ball must sit within the quarter-circle at the nearest corner flag. Players from the defending team cannot approach within 10 yards (9.1m) of the ball until it is in play (i.e. until it has moved the distance of its own circumference). A goal can be scored direct from a corner.

The ball is in play even...

...if it has rebounded from the frame of the goal or corner flag into the field of play

...if it rebounds from a linesman or referee into the field of play

...if there appears to have been a breach of the rules, until a decision is given by the referee

Equipment

Bargain buys

To play competitive football you will need to invest in two items of equipment (three if you are a goalkeeper), but even these need not be expensive. There are always bargains available to the discerning shopper, providing you have no objection to wearing footwear endorsed by a fallen idol, or shinpads in last season's colour.

Footwear

Footwear is the most important item of equipment for a footballer. If your boots are uncomfortable or ill-fitting you will not strike the ball properly and running will soon become painful. However, this does not mean that every amateur player should spend a fortune on the latest kangaroo-skin boots. Even relatively inexpensive footwear can be extremely comfortable, providing you choose well and look after your purchase.

When buying a pair of boots, it is essential to take your time. Try on as many different brands as you can - even those you are initially not keen on. Eventually you will find a pair that fit you, both in terms of width and length. You must also consider the type of pitches you will be playing on, as this will determine what type of sole you opt for. Football boots come in four main types:

Moulded

The sole and studs on moulded boots are made from one piece of rubber. The studs are usually short and closely spaced. Moulded boots are best for hard pitches, although those with longer studs are satisfactory on softer ground.

Screw-in studs

Traditionally, screw-in boots have just six studs, each stud screwing directly into the sole of the boot. The great advantage of this system is that you can change your studs to suit the conditions (i.e. long, metal studs for soft pitches and short, rubber studs for firm ground).

Cleats/blades boots

A recent innovation on the part of football boot manufacturers is the cleat-sole boot. These boots are based on designs used in American sports (most notably baseball). In theory these boots, which have a one-piece sole that is made up of a series of blades or cleats, can be used on both firm and soft ground.

Football's enduring appeal and international popularity owes much to the fact that it is a sport that makes no discrimination on economic grounds. Expensive equipment, fancy clothing and vast areas of land are not needed to enjoy a game of football. A ball, some rudimentary goalposts and a few willing souls are all that's required to partake in the world's best-loved game.

Astro-turf

The arrival of the first astro-turf pitches in the early 1980s saw the invention of a special type of boot, specifically for this surface. Astro pitches are no longer used at the top level of the game, but the boots are still made to meet the demands of amateur footballers. Astro boots look more like training shoes than football boots, and have a sole that is covered in small studs (often no more than a 0.5cm in diameter).

Shin pads

Football is one of only a few contact sports that are played without padding and body armour. A footballer's only real protection from injury is a pair of shinpads. The Laws of the game now include shinguards as part of the compulsory equipment for a player. Any player who does not wear shinguards during a match can be asked to leave the field. But it is not just against the rules to play without pads; it is also against common sense. So use your head and wear a pair of pads. The best ones come with integral ankle pads and socks.

Goalkeeper's gloves

Back in the 1960s a keeper's only aid to catching the ball was a pair of green cotton gloves. Today, the modern goalie looking for a pair of gloves will find a bewildering array of designs, each claiming some spurious scientific advantage over the others. The bottom line, however, is to opt for a pair that feel comfortable and that offer enough padding to help absorb the impact of a shot.

Paraphernalia

Be warned, the marketing departments of sportwear firms are constantly on the look out for new gimmicks and gizmos that will supposedly make you become a better player. Most of these inventions and innovations will disappear into the ether. Stick to the basics and leave the titanium-soled football boots and carbon-fibre nose clips to those that get paid to wear them.

Glossary

A

Aerobic training
The aim of aerobic training is to increase the flow of oxygen to the muscles. Endurance training such as swimming is an excellent example.

Anaerobic training
Exercise 'without air', (i.e. high intensity activity, for example weight-lifting and sprinting). Anaerobic training can only be maintained for short spells.

B

Banana kick
Free-kick, often associated with Brazilian football. The ball is bent around the defensive wall and into the corner of the net.

C

Carbohydrates (complex)
Slow-burning fuel for the human body. It's the most important part of an athlete's diet. Carbohydrate is stored in the liver and muscles as glycogen until being converted into glucose during exercise. Good sources of complex carbohydrate include pasta, rice, bananas and cereals.

Carbohydrates (simple)
Fast-burning fuel for the body. Simple carbs are commonly found in sugary food. They provide a short-term increase in energy level but do not provide any sustained gain. They should be taken to complement complex carbohydrates, not to replace them.

Closing down
Defensive technique used to deny opponents time and space.

Cruyff turn
An attacking move first used by Holland's legendary forward Johan Cruyff.

D

Diamond
A tactical system which employs four midfielders: one attacking midfielder to support the strikers; one defensive midfielder to take the ball from the defence; and two wide midfielders who 'tuck in' to protect the full-backs.

Diuretic
Substances which cause increased output of urine. Diuretics should never be consumed at half-time. Coffee, tea and alcohol are all diuretics.

F

Flat back-four
A strategic formation, 4-4-2, in which the defence consists of two centre-backs and two full-backs who play in a line.

G

Glycogen
Sugar is stored in this form in the liver and muscles. Glycogen is converted to glucose during exercise and is burned in the muscle cells to produce energy.

H

High-intensity training
Training intended to keep the heart rate at a level similar to that reached during a competitive match. This type of exercise should be complemented by sessions of moderate and low intensity, during which players work below their maximum capacity.

I

Isotonic drinks (right)
Easily absorbed into the blood stream, an isotonic solution provides quick rehydration. A simple isotonic drink can be made by mixing fruit juice and water in equal measures.

L

Lactic tolerance
Lactic acid builds up in the muscles during activity as glucose is burnt in the muscle cells. A build up of lactate causes muscle pain. The

length of time (and the extent of pain) which an athlete can endure and still continue to exercise is his lactate tolerance level.

Ligaments
Tough, fibrous tissues which link to the bone and reinforce the joint. Ligaments keep the joints in place while allowing great flexibility. Ligament injuries are common in football. It can take a great deal of time and rest for a ligament to regain its strength and flexibility once damaged.

O

Overlap
An overlap is a run made off the ball, usually down the wing. The runner makes his run from behind the ball, getting ahead of the ball, which is held by a team-mate who releases it in front of the runner.

P

Plyometric training (opposite)
Training which develops explosive power within the muscles. Examples of plyometric training include jumping over hurdles and running across benches.

Power to weight ratio
This is an individual's muscle power as against his overall body weight. Muscle is very heavy and at a certain point it becomes inefficient (for footballers) to build and carry extra muscle.

Proteins
This is the main component of muscle and it is vital for growth. Protein takes a long time to digest and, contrary to popular belief, is not a major source of energy. A healthy diet will consist of more carbohydrate than protein.

S

Sweeper
Defensive position which refers to the last player in a central-defensive trio. A sweeper usually plays alongside two markers and is responsible for patrolling the area behind his two colleagues. He is also expected to carry the ball out from the back.

T

Tendons
Tendons are linking agents which join muscles to bone.

The trap
The basic method of controlling a football using the foot.

W

Warm down
A short period of gentle exercise (similar to a warm-up) should be followed after every match. This will help break down any lactate which has built up in the muscles during exercise.

Warm-up
A warm-up should be carried out prior to any exercise. It is intended to raise the heart rate prior to competitive exertion and warm the muscles to make them more supple.

Wing-back
Variation on the full-back position. Wing-backs are usually used in a 3-5-2 or 5-3-2 system. They are responsible for patrolling the flanks and are expected to spend a great deal of the game attacking. However, they must also defend their wing when required, and as a result this is a stamina-sapping position.

Z

Zonal marking
Tactical system in which players are responsible for defending areas of the pitch rather than for marking particular players.

index

Picture acknowledgements

Holland & Barrett /Healthy Magazine 10 Bottom

Octopus Publishing Group Ltd. /Richard Francis Front Endpaper, Back Endpaper , 6, 14 Top, 14 Bottom Left, 14 Bottom Right, 20 Top, 20 Centre, 20 Bottom, 21 Top, 21 Centre, 21 Bottom Right, 22 left, 22 Centre Centre Left, 22 Centre Centre Right, 22 Centre Right, 23 Top, 23 Bottom, 24, 25 Top, 25 Bottom, 26 Main Picture, 26 Top Left, 26 Bottom Right, 27 Top Left, 27 Bottom Right, 28, 29, 31 Top Left, 31 Top Right, 31 Bottom Right, 32 Bottom Left, 32 Bottom Centre, 32 Bottom Right, 33 Centre, 33 Bottom, 36 Centre Right, 36 Bottom, 37, 38 right, 38 Centre, 39 Top, 39 Bottom Left, 39 Bottom Right, 41 Bottom Left, 41 Bottom Centre, 41 Bottom Right, 42 Top Left, 42 Top Centre, 44 Top, 44 Centre, 44 Bottom, 45 Top, 45 Bottom, 47 Bottom Left, 47 Bottom Centre, 47 Bottom Right, 49 Top, 49 Centre, 49 Bottom, 72 Top, 72 Centre, 72 Bottom, 73 Top, 73 Centre, 73 Bottom, 104 Top, 104 Centre, 104 Bottom, 105 Top, 105 Centre, 105 Bottom, 107 Top, 107 Centre, 107 Bottom, 109 Top, 109 Bottom, 114, 115 left, 115 right, 117 Top, 117 Bottom, 124 Bottom, 124 Top, 125, 126 Top, 126 Bottom, 127 right, 127 Centre, 127 left 133, 154, 155 /Alex Henderson Front Cover, 1, 2-3, 8-9, 34-35, 36, 42 Bottom Centre, 42 Bottom Right, 43 left, 43 right, 50 left, 50 right, 50 Centre, 51 Top, 51 Bottom, 52, 54 Top, 54 Centre Left, 54 Centre, 54 Centre Right, 55 Top Left, 55 Top Centre, 55 Top Right, 55 Bottom, 56 Top Left, 56 Top Centre, 56 Top Right, 56 Bottom, 57 Top Left, 57 Top Centre Left, 57 Top Centre Right, 57 Top Right, 57 Bottom Left, 57 Bottom Centre, 57 Bottom Right, 58 Top Left, 58 Top Right, 58 Bottom Left, 58 Bottom Right, 59 Top Left, 59 Top Right, 59 Bottom Left, 59 Bottom Right, 61 Top Left, 61 Top Right, 61 Bottom Left, 61 Bottom Right, 62 right, 62 Top Left, 62 Centre Left, 62 Centre Right, 63 left, 63 right, 63 Centre Left, 63 Centre Right, 64 Top Left, 64 Top Right, 64 Bottom Left, 64 Bottom Right, 65 right, 65 Top, 65 Centre, 66 Bottom Left, 66-67, 66-67 Bottom, 68-69, 74 Top Left, 74 Top Right, 74 Bottom, 75 Top Left, 75 Top Centre, 75 Top Right, 75 Bottom Left, 75 Bottom Centre, 75 Bottom Right, 76 Top Left, 76 Top Right, 76 Centre Left, 76 Centre Right, 76 Bottom, 77 Top, 77 Top Centre, 77 Bottom, 77 Bottom Centre, 78 Top, 78 Centre, 78 Bottom, 79 Top, 79 Bottom, 80 Top, 80 Centre, 80 Bottom, 81 Top, 81 Centre, 81 Bottom, 82-83, 85 Bottom, 86 left, 86 right, 87 left, 87 right, 88 Top, 88 Top Centre, 88 Centre, 88 Bottom, 89 Top, 89 Bottom, 89 Bottom Centre, 90 Top, 90 Centre, 90 Bottom, 91 Top, 91 Centre, 91 Bottom, 92 left, 92 right, 92 Centre, 94, 94 Centre, 94 Bottom, 96 left, 96 right, 97 left, 97 right, 98, 99 left, 99 right, 100 Top, 100 Centre, 100 Bottom, 101 Top, 101 Top Centre, 101 Bottom, 101 Bottom Centre, 102-103, 106, 110 Top, 110 Centre, 110 Bottom, 111 Top, 111 Bottom, 112 Top, 112 Bottom, 113 Top Left, 113 Top Right, 113 Bottom Left, 122-123, 134-135, 144-145, 151 /David Jordan 11 Centre /Sue Jorgensen 11 Top /Hilary Moore 10 /Clive Streeter 12/Philip Webb 11 Bottom /Trevor Wood 13 Bottom

Umbro /152-153

Special Photography:
Octopus Publishing Group Ltd. /Tessa Musgrave 16, 17 Top, 17 Centre, 17 Bottom, 18, 19, 47 Top Left, 47 Top Centre, 47 Top Right, 48 left, 48 right, 48 Centre, 70, 71 Top, 71 Centre, 84 left, 84 right, 84 Centre, 85 Top, 85 Centre, 93 Top, 93 Top Centre, 93 Bottom, 93 Bottom Centre, 95, 108, 120 Top, 120 Bottom, 121 Centre Left, 121 Centre Right, 121 Bottom Left, 121 Bottom Right, 129 Top, 129 Centre, 129 Bottom, 148 left, 148 right, 149, 150

All cover pictures:
Alex Henderson except for bottom, centre left from **Tessa Musgrave**

Artworks:
Kevin Jones Associates